DATE

Controlling
Overhead

CONTROLLING OVERHEAD

by

HARRY TIPPER, Jr.

AMERICAN MANAGEMENT ASSOCIATION

To
Harry Tipper, Sr.

dynamic executive
inspiring teacher
author of business books

who sought to instill in his son
the art of being an executive

Preface

This book is intended for businessmen—executives, managers of profit centers, and those who aspire to such positions. It is concerned primarily with overhead as a management problem, and with the problems of managing overhead. Its interests are those of the man who must do something about the costs of overhead, rather than those of specialists in cost analysis, systems, and industrial engineering who may be called in to assist in developing information about overhead. As such, it is neither by nor for accountants (although it will be of interest to those of that profession who are involved in the broader questions of internal financial management).

The approach to overhead control developed in this book is not that of any one company; rather, it is based on practices of many companies as described to the author by their officials, as reported in case studies, and as gathered from experiences in working out the problems of a number

7

of companies of all sizes. Many executives, I believe, would subscribe to the philosophy behind it. It is intended to provide a balanced executive approach to control of overhead which any company can adopt. With such a point of view as this, a company can provide methodology to fit its own requirements.

HARRY TIPPER, JR.

Contents

PART I: The Problem of Overhead 13
Why Overhead Is a Special Problem . . 16
Controllable Overhead 24
The Nature of Overhead 29
Overhead Staffing 35
Paying for Overhead 41
Essentiality of Overhead Functions . . 50

PART II: A Program for Controlling Overhead . . 63
Objectives of Overhead Control 64
Executive Attitude Toward Overhead
Control 67
Planning Overhead Control 71
Reorganization of Procedures 80
Use of Staff in Overhead Control . . . 93
Authorization of Overhead Expenses . . 97
Elimination of Positions 103
Supervision of Overhead 106
Overhead Profit Center 116
Some Conclusions 119

About the Author 125

PART I

THE PROBLEM OF OVERHEAD

I

It is scarcely possible to write about overhead without using accounting terminology. It is desirable, therefore, to have common understanding of terms used throughout this book.

We will not be concerned with the nuances of such terms. Indeed, they are likely to take on special connotations within single companies, according to the practices each develops in regard to individual charges. Fine differences in definitions can be left to those who are expert in them. We need only enough understanding of them to be able to apply general principles to many companies.

The term *overhead*, as used in the title and throughout this book, is meant in the generic sense. When applied broadly, it is understood to mean burden or indirect costs of all kinds in a company, at whatever organizational level they are charged. In large companies, overhead is charged

13

at cost centers and profit centers. Overhead not so charged is called herein *general overhead*. A *cost center* is taken to mean:

> A division, a department or subdivision thereof, a group of machines or of men or of both, a single machine and its operating force, or any other unit of activity into which a manufacturing plant and its operations are divided for purposes of cost assignment and allocation.[1]

A cost center, then, is a subdivision of a profit center. Its overhead includes, for instance, its supervision and such manufacturing support functions as scheduling. There may be several tiers of cost centers within a large manufacturing operation.

A *profit center* includes not only the manufacturing costs charged to its cost centers but also selling costs, the costs of its own general management, and the share of general overhead allocated to it, if the practice within the company is to make such allocation. When revenue derived from its selling activities is credited to it, its own profit can be calculated.

Performance of a cost center is usually measured in terms of its cost and output. In its periodic performance reports or operating statements, the cost of the quantities produced in the period is stated, normally, as an average unit cost. This unit cost and its composition are invaluable

---

[1] This and other quoted definitions are taken from Eric L. Kohler, *A Dictionary for Accountants*, Prentice-Hall, Inc., Englewood Cliffs, N.J., 1963.

indices of performance, both to the immediate managers of the cost centers themselves and to their superiors. By this means, an objective indicator of performance is obtained, and managers at all levels have a common understanding of its meaning and importance. Because of the value of such performance reports, they are an important aspect of accounting, and much attention has been given to increasing their significance.

Performance of a profit center is measured as if it were an independent company. A *pro forma* profit and loss statement is made up for it from which profits can be compared month to month. The hypothetical aspects of such statements are understood in the companies that use them, but any disadvantages are outweighed by their great usefulness.

In many companies the costs of sales departments are treated as if they were cost centers; that is, costs are compared per unit sold or per dollar of sales. Although the relationship between cost and sales is more tenuous than between cost and product, it is valuable to relate them, especially when there is sufficient history behind the figures.

Overhead costs are usually classified by, and charged to, overhead pools. Such pools are ordinarily functional organizational units, such as accounting, advertising, and auditing. In theory, "classification of overhead costs begins with the determination of responsibilities of cost incurrence." In actuality, as you will see in this book, responsibility for such costs is not where it appears to be and is not always easily determined.

15

At first glance, "controllable" and "noncontrollable" overhead as the terms are used here may be confused with the fixed and variable costs of accountancy. A *fixed cost* is "an expenditure that does not vary with business volume; e.g., interest on bonds." A *variable cost* is "an operating cost or operating costs as a class that vary directly, sometimes proportionately, with production; e.g., materials consumed." The distinction drawn here is between costs that management has some chance of improving and those it can scarcely hope to do much about. As we are concerned with controlling overhead, attention focuses on areas of overhead where control can be the more fruitful.

Finally, a distinction is made between managers and executives. The different roles of these two classifications are a topic wholly separate from that of this book. In relation to the present subject, it is enough to say that *managers* may be responsible for any and all classes of costs but one; only *executives* can be responsible for general overhead.

Why Overhead Is a Special Problem

Controlling overhead costs is a special problem in management. It cannot be delegated away like most problems. For one thing, there are no firm criteria to measure how the delegation is to be handled. The difference between enough, too little, and too much is a matter of judgment. Judgment of overhead is greatly influenced by the point of view. The same costs will seem too much to the manager of a profit center, to whom overhead is allocated, and too little to the head of an overhead function who must satisfy demands on his services.

Control of production costs or selling costs is being delegated more or less successfully all the time. Those to whom control is delegated understand how their performance will be judged. They know that they themselves and their superiors will use the same criteria and will interpret them in the same way. The production manager and his superior have a common desire to reduce unit costs. The sales manager and his superior have a like incentive to improve the ratio of selling costs to volume.

The head of an overhead function can be expected to operate within his budget. He and his superior, however, have differing motives. He is interested in supplying more service, counsel, and information to the other departments, in being a greater influence in the company—in other words, in obtaining a larger budget. His superior, on the other hand, is well aware that overhead is a deduction from profit. He wants to constrain overhead budgets and generate larger profits.

Control of overhead, therefore, is a different problem from controlling production or selling costs. Different motivations and attitudes are at work. It requires a different type of management and control. Supervising the performance of overhead functions requires different skills and standards from those used to evaluate the profitability of profit-making divisions.

Production men quickly learn from experience, if they have not already learned in theory, how a change in their costs for materials or labor changes their unit costs. They can see the direct relationships that prevail between the costs they control and the costs of the things they make. They know that they will be able to measure in their performance figures next month a reduction they make today in crew size or amount of materials consumed. They have learned, in the same direct manner, the effect a variation in volume has on their unit cost figures.

The very disciplines of manufacturing lead to optimization of the relationships between direct costs and profits. All the thinking of production men is geared to the idea of maximum utilization of plant. They want to manufacture as much product as possible with the resources available to them. They feel achievement in establishing new records of output. They try to reduce wastage and idle time of men and machines below previous records.

Watching their performance figures has reinforced these disciplines. Production men have learned how their elements of costs, volume, and unit cost are tied together; in a drive to increase output, for instance, they have learned how careless wastage of materials can wipe out part of the anticipated gains in unit cost. They realize that they must trim payrolls as soon as production is cut back, much as they hate to do so.

Even in the area of supporting manufacturing services (provided such services are charged to their performance figures) production men see the direct relationship between charges and unit costs. They understand that their performance will look worse if they add an engineer unless he makes compensatory savings in utilization of plant, labor, or materials. Hence manufacturing services are always looking for ways to reduce the labor content of product, to get more output from plant, and to lessen materials consumption.

When businesses do get into trouble because of expenses attributable to manufacturing, it is most often because of lack of control over inventory. Overbuying and overproduction and overinvestment in plant affect the financial condition of a company, but they do not affect production performance figures adversely.

In overhead areas, there is no such clear relationship between expenses and profits as exists in production. The effect of manufacturing costs on profits is obvious down to the level of each cost center; the effect of overhead expenses on profit is apparent only in aggregate. Changes in costs are evident only in the rate of overhead applied, and the reasons for these changes are usually to be found only by intensive investigation. Consequently, personnel in overhead categories have no such direct profit motivation as exists in manufacturing.

No company, furthermore, adds a vice president, an accountant, or a research scientist with the expectation that he will effect compensatory savings in overhead to improve profits next month. Whereas a production engineer may be added in the expectation that he will find ways to eliminate the need, say, for three machine operators, there is no thought that an additional vice president will save his salary in clerks. As we all know, quite the reverse is likely to be the case; he, in turn, will tend to raise other overhead expenses.

The justification for hiring a production engineer is to

reduce costs. In adding a vice president, an accountant, or a research scientist, it is obvious that overhead costs will be increased, not reduced. Consequently, the justification here has to be that the growth pattern of the company is such that an increase in total overhead dollars will not increase the overhead rate. When total overhead dollars increase faster than sales, this increase can only be at the expense of profits.

Control of general overhead must be initiated at the executive level. In the eyes of stockholders, responsibility for net profit rests on the chief executive, and the last deduction that determines net profit before taxes is the aggregate of general overhead. Control of general overhead cannot be delegated away to managers of overhead pools because the chief executive has the final responsibility for balancing the expenditures of pools so that their aggregate is not an excessive deduction from profit. Control of production costs can be delegated to the level of cost centers, but control of overhead can be delegated to pool levels only after total overhead dollars are controlled. Those dollars, in turn, can be broken down to pools for control and measurement of the expenses of functional units.

With this relationship between aggregate overhead and profit, there is a widespread tendency to justify overhead as a percentage of sales. As a consequence, those in charge of overhead pools tend to support their costs in terms of a percentage of sales. It is quite common for individual companies to report, for instance, the percentage of sales going into advertising or research.

Such thinking, however, is just the opposite to that of

the production man. He is looking for ways to reduce costs of manufacture and to lower his unit costs. The manager of an overhead pool is looking for ways to maintain a ratio of overhead expenses to sales. Efforts of the former increase profits while those of the latter tend to freeze profit margins in growth situations and to reduce them in declining markets.

Indeed, for many companies the so-called cost-price squeeze is a misnomer. More properly, they are in an overhead-profit squeeze. This fact is borne out if manufacturing cost and overhead are plotted in relation to sales over a number of years: It is likely to be the case that overhead expenses increase more rapidly than sales, thereby eroding profit margins.

In general, overhead expenses do not relate to volume as they are expected to. In theory, overhead should decline, as a ratio of sales, when volume increases. For most companies, however, the long-term trend is not toward a smaller percentage, in spite of general growth. This is equivalent to saying that we have not learned how to operate more efficiently in overhead areas with increasing size. Any comparison of large with small companies in the same fields will support this conclusion. The smaller companies will have relatively lower overheads, although they may also have relatively higher manufacturing costs.

Overheads are the most difficult areas to control in any reversal of growth patterns. In a long-term study of one large company (see Exhibit 1), overhead expenses were found to have continued to rise, albeit slowly, all through the thirties, even though sales and manufacturing costs

21

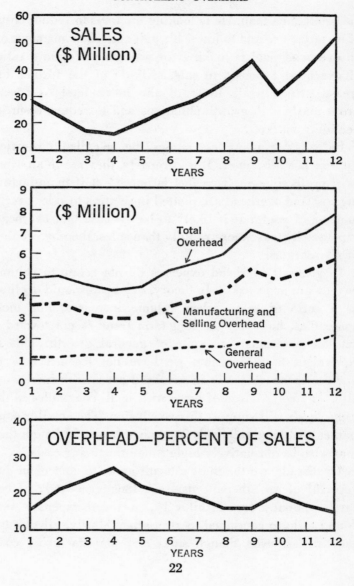

EXHIBIT 1

THE CURIOUS BEHAVIOR OF OVERHEAD
UNDER DEPRESSED CONDITIONS

In this actual case, depicted in graph form on the facing page, sales declined 46 percent in four years. Manufacturing support and selling costs dropped by 15 percent in the same period. Although the rise in general overhead was checked for one year, coincident with the bottom in sales, it was never again to be as low as it had been at the earlier peak.

It took seven years for sales to exceed the earlier record (by 1 percent), and the same length of time for manufacturing support and selling costs (by 7 percent). In the same seven years, general overhead increased by 51 percent and total overhead by 17 percent. By the eighth year, sales were up, and the total overhead rate was back in line at 16 percent.

In the twelfth year, sales—up by 74 percent—were heading into new high ground. Total overhead had grown by only 63 percent, the 87 percent increase in general overhead being compensated for by the lower 55 percent increase in manufacturing support and selling costs. Overhead rate had dropped one percentage point.

The lesson of the hard years had been learned. When sales fell in the tenth year, overhead was cut back. Control was imposed in all categories of expense. When sales turned up again the next year, overhead rate returned to a satisfactory level.

declined sharply. This trend reflects the tendency of management to try to control through the staff instead of directly on the line.

From all these considerations, then, it is apparent that controlling overhead is a special problem. It should not be approached in the same way as is used in controlling manufacturing costs. Too often, management waits until the overhead-profit squeeze becomes critical before acting. Under such conditions, the meat ax is used, and a general directive is issued to cut all departments by a set percentage. In the process, fat is trimmed where it exists, but blood is drawn, also, in areas where the tendency to build empires has been resisted. It is not necessary to wait to control overhead, but it is a very difficult thing to accomplish on any organized and consistent basis. Nevertheless, there is no other management activity more directly related to profit making.

Controllable Overhead

The term *overhead*, as used in accountancy, means essentially any charge which cannot be attributed exclusively to a single salable product or service. Charges which must be prorated or allocated to several products or services are in the overhead category whether applied, for accounting purposes, before or after manufacturing cost.

When we look at overhead expenses from the point of view of general management, however, we see that accounting practices are not precisely relevant. Many line items of overhead cannot be "managed" in any usual sense of the word. Neither executives nor managers can control them;

the dollar amount of such items cannot be modified, upward or downward, by management of the internal organization.

Such an item, for example, is the real estate tax on a plant. The amount of such tax is properly in overhead. Management is "responsible" for it. By community, legal, or political actions, management may even be able to influence it favorably. Nevertheless, the amount charged to a plant for local real estate tax is by no means amenable to the same sort of management review, analysis, and control as are many other items of overhead.

By way of contrast, such an item as production engineering in the same plant is a "manageable" category of expense. It can be reviewed, analyzed, budgeted, and controlled by appropriate managers. It can even reflect the ability of managers to stimulate superior performance in subordinates so that the function is performed more effectively; hence the amount charged to production engineering expense is truly a controllable charge.

Thus we see that there are controllable and noncontrollable overhead items. Noncontrollable overhead in a particular company may include such costs as:

- Real estate taxes.
- Royalties, paid and received.
- State franchise, sales, and income taxes.
- Commissions, paid and received.
- Bad debt and other reserves.
- Insurance premiums.
- Debt service.

In brief, any charge imposed by a regulatory body or made

to fulfill a long-term agreement can be considered non-controllable in the sense used here. Such charges are not subject to normal managerial purview and action through the internal organization, even though management retains responsibility and must continue to scrutinize them.

All other categories of overhead can be regarded as controllable. However, they are not all subject to the same type of managerial control, and they can be managed at different organizational levels. Even though the same principles of control will apply to them all, it is well to distinguish between them.

Manufacturing overhead. It is common practice to apply charges attributable to direct support of manufacturing at the level of cost or profit centers. By this means, managerial responsibility for such indirect charges is unified with responsibility for direct costs. Control of overhead is decentralized in parallel with control of direct costs. Line control of costs is strengthened. Both the direct and the indirect charges they can control appear in the performance figures of managers of these centers. Hence these indirect costs are subject to the same type of control as production men apply to their direct costs.

Long-term data seem to warrant the conclusion that manufacturing costs (direct and indirect costs of manufacturing) show a significantly more favorable relationship to sales than does general overhead.[2] This relationship

---

[2] The same conclusion can be drawn from "productivity" trends which many companies watch closely. In these days of automation, however, productivity as such should be regarded as a composite of direct and indirect labor, supervision, and capital employed.

has led to the conclusion that the cost-price squeeze is often an overhead-profit squeeze. That is, the tendency of manufacturing costs to hold or decline as a percentage of sales is more than offset in the growth of general overhead.

Selling costs. As with their treatment of expenses for manufacturing support, many companies unify responsibility for selling costs in the sales organization. Unfortunately, accounting systems can only provide a method of accumulating such expenses. They do not give a measure of cost versus effectiveness, such as is provided in statements of manufacturing cost. Every step in manufacturing is carefully planned to contribute to the value of product. The cost accounting system provides a good measurement of the effectiveness with which each step is accomplished. There may be equally careful planning of the selling effort, but there can be no absolute measure of the contribution advertising, travel, entertainment, and customer service make to sales. Only historical trends in the ratio of expense to sales can give an appreciation of accomplishment. Beyond the accumulation of costs, measurements must be developed outside the general accounting system or as supplementary to it.

Nevertheless, segregation of all expenses attributable to the marketing effort accomplishes several things:

1. Managerial responsibility for selling costs is unified with responsibility for performance of sales.
2. Such responsibility is decentralized to control levels below those where general overhead is controlled.
3. Line control of costs and results is strengthened.

27

These measures result in effective control of selling expenses. Surprisingly enough, historical data suggest that we have been even more effective in controlling these costs than we have in controlling manufacturing costs. Restated, this means that while our manufacturing costs per sales dollar are now slightly lower, our selling costs are significantly lower than they were in earlier periods with which we can make comparisons.

The reasons are not far to seek: Markets have been growing. At the same time, customers have been getting larger. In many areas of business, a larger market is concentrated in fewer companies. The automotive market is representative of many others. If you sell to automobile manufacturers, there are fewer companies to contact now than there were. Each company buys in larger volume. A single purchase order from one of them now may well be for several times as many dollars as would a similar order 10 or 20 years ago. Therefore, the ratio of selling costs to sales at present is likely to compare favorably with past experience.

General overhead. For purposes of managerial control, all other controllable overhead expenses may be classified as general overhead. Such overhead is brought into the profit system only at the executive level; that is to say, responsibility for its gross effect on profit is unified in the executive. No subordinate profit center can be responsible for general overhead because a subordinate manager cannot be held responsible, for example, for the salary and expenses of the chief executive. In principle, therefore, this responsibility is not delegable.

The Problem

We can except from this statement any parts of general overhead which are charged to subordinate profit centers on the basis of actual use, *provided,* however, that the subordinate manager in fact has complete control over such use in the same way he does of his other costs. If he is not equally free to use or not to use competing outside services, any responsibility attributed to him for parts of general overhead is fictional to a degree.

Many companies can attest that general overhead is principally to blame for the overhead-profit squeeze. It is in this area, therefore, that we will be most concerned with principles of overhead control.

The Nature of Overhead

Except in the special case of noncontrollable overhead, the bulk of overhead expenses is related to people. Normally, from 65 percent to 85 percent of the total cost in overhead functions is related to people. The lower percentage will pertain, for instance, to a function such as testing, where there may be a considerable investment in plant. An even lower percentage may occur in some companies where expenditures on advertising are a significant portion of the sales dollar. The higher percentage will apply in such functions as, for example, an internal legal or personnel department where there is little need for equipment and where costs are concentrated in salaries.

In general, however, overhead functions are mostly services performed by people. Practices vary between companies as to the amount of such services procured from outside as against those supplied from inside. In any case, only a small proportion of overhead expenses is for expenditures and depreciation. The major proportion is for salaries and wages. Most of the rest of overhead expenses is directly proportional to payroll; for instance, fringe benefits, travel, telephone, office space, light, heat and power, stationery and supplies, depreciation of furniture and fixtures.

Consequently, a significant change in overhead means a change in the number of people performing overhead functions. The normal approach to overhead control—issuing instructions to curtail toll telephone calls, requiring prior approval for travel, and so on—merely skirts the issue. In most companies even a large percentage reduction in overhead telephone and travel charges can scarcely be detected in the overhead rate. For real accomplishment in this area, therefore, it is necessary to confront the problem of people.

This is most difficult for any company. Most companies face up to it only when a significant drop in volume sends overhead rates skyward. Under such circumstances, drastic action becomes necessary. Either or both of two courses are taken:

1. Expenses of all functions are required to be cut by edict (often by 10 percent).
2. The company is reorganized.

In either case, overhead expenses are cut by reducing the number of people in overhead categories. It is noteworthy, however, that such approaches to overhead control are only partially effective.

First, results are usually temporary at best. As soon as pressure is relaxed, overhead tends to climb again. If relaxation of pressure is coincident with recovery of volume, overhead tends to increase *above* the previous peak, indicating the temporary nature of corrective actions.

Second, reduction of expenses is likely to be more severe in areas of manufacturing support and selling expenses than in the general overhead categories. If such be the case, the ability of the company to reduce costs and strengthen marketing is impaired. The profit-making parts of the company are weakened, and line is downgraded in relation to staff.

We can develop at least some of the reasons why these patterns tend to appear in the history of many companies. In times of stress when profits disappear, control over decentralized profit centers normally is tightened by the executive. Costs at lower levels are reviewed more thoroughly, actions scrutinized more closely, and performance analyzed more carefully. Since the same span of management is in effect, the executive must turn to supporting staff to perform these activities. Because assignments given to staff to meet the crisis are over and above their normal functions, the staff load actually tends to increase as the company reacts to stress. There is only a minor slackening of normal activities by staff when these special assignments are laid on them. Since it is their normal inclination to want to take over line functions, staff will relinquish their new special assignments reluctantly, if at all, when the crisis has passed.

As a consequence of these factors, reduction in general

overhead is minimized when there is stress on the company. Unless the executive is exceptionally alert, the crisis may result in a permanent shift of some expenses into the category of general overhead and an incremental increase in total overhead.

Within decentralized profit centers, meanwhile, double pressures are at work. There is the normal discipline of periodic performance figures which are showing unfavorable results. These figures are demanding local action to control costs and to reduce expenses of supporting services. This discipline is reinforced by pressure, exerted in the name of the executive, for further action along the same lines. Because of intensified staff activity, this pressure is far more detailed and pointed than was customary in previous reviews of performance. It is probably fortified by directed reductions which were not attempted before when things were going well.

It is far more difficult to apply the same discipline and pressure at the executive level to general overhead. A much greater diversity of functions is involved. Operation of company procedures requires use of those functions. Consequently, an appreciable reduction of general overhead seldom comes about without substantial reorganization in which established procedures are reformed. This is a drastic process and one which managements shy away from, quite understandably.

In theory, at least, control of overhead should be part of the company planning process. Nevertheless, it is very much easier to resolve to carry out a plan of overhead control than it is to adhere to it consistently over the years.

Such a plan would have little value unless it were implemented. It would produce little benefit if it were not carried out over a long period of time, perhaps over more than one executive regime.

If planning devolves into just another staff function, furthermore, it is likely to become increasingly preoccupied with the methodology of planning and further removed from reality. Too often it leads to a situation where various overhead functions are justified on fixed percentages of volume. Hypothetical formulas are established which, with usage, acquire an artificial validity. Many companies, in fact, already report annual expenses for research or advertising as a percentage of sales as if this were an indication of progressive management.

Unfortunately, there is no way of relating the essentiality of overhead functions to a ratio of sales. If it were possible, business would long since have developed a rule which said, for instance, that for every $10 million of sales you should have 0.8 lawyers, 1.3 internal auditors, and so on.

Likewise, efforts to justify levels of overhead expenses on the basis of comparative practices should be treated with reserve. No doubt it would be of interest, say, to a machine tool builder to know how many copywriters and freight routers other machine tool builders have. Such information, however, would not tell him whether it is better to be average, below average, or above average. Since his product lines and mix will differ from those of other machine tool builders, practice in the industry may mislead him.

In spite of these considerations, there should be planning of overhead control. While planning in respect to manufacturing support and selling expenses can be decentralized, planning for general overhead is, by its nature, an executive responsibility because of the relationship between overhead and profit: The earnings the company expects to be able to report and the dividends it expects to be able to declare will be influenced directly by its overhead.

An executive can carry out such planning himself only in the aggregate. That is to say, he can keep a projection of total overhead expenses over the next several years which he has worked out in relation to projected sales. He can delegate to supporting staff the elaboration of his projection in terms of individual overhead categories. He can require staff to monitor performance for him against his projection.

Most important, he will have to review requests for new or expanded overhead functions in light of his forecast. It is in this last respect that so many attempts at overhead planning fall down.

He must continually evaluate the need for consistent application of his plan against pressures exerted on him for additional services and expenditures. Every sort of rationalization will be used to make him deviate from his plan: the improved economic outlook, recovery of lost markets, greater profitability, the precedence of competitive action, economies to be gained from a new service, overloading of present staff, image of the company. These arguments, furthermore, will be those not of strange salesmen but of his closest associates and most trusted counselors. It will take all his vision and fortitude to resist such blandishments, if he is indeed able to do so at all. This is the price he must pay, however, if he is to have planned control of overhead. It is no wonder that not many companies have consistent performance in this area. On the other hand, there are many companies which, in the course of their history, have suffered because they lacked overhead control.

It is in the very nature of overhead that it is difficult to control. There are no firm criteria by which to analyze it, except when the total cost of overhead eats too deeply into profits. Nevertheless, there is scarcely another area of management where executive attention can be more richly rewarded.

Overhead Staffing

Because of the relationship between people and overhead expenses, policies and practices in regard to staffing have a direct bearing on control of overhead. This is not merely a question of salary administration or personnel development. It is basically a reflection of executive attitude toward control of overhead expenses.

As far as employees in the various functions are concerned, there is a fundamental difference in attitude between most of those in staff and those in line functions. In production functions it is normal to staff both wage and salary positions for the minimum average expected in line loading. If there is a surge in line loading—for instance, to make month-end shipments—the production manager will expect to handle it with his regular crew, possibly with some overtime. Furthermore, all his subordinates will look on that as a normal staffing program. They will seek ways of getting past peaks without adding employees.

Only when orders are consistently beyond the capacity of his regular crews, even putting in overtime, will he increase the size of his crews or add to the number of shifts. His reinforced crews, in turn, become his normal staffing to handle a higher level of orders. Added load is spread over salaried workers as much as possible, and production support is increased only as schedules show a consistently higher level of orders and the workload is clearly beyond the capacity of existing staff.

In the same way with the sales force, one salesman is expected to handle a territory until such time as demand in that territory can support two salesmen. The territory is not staffed on the basis that two customers may want to see a salesman at the same time. One salesman is expected to handle such situations as best he can, or to call on his territorial manager to support him. Only when he has more business than he can handle himself will he want to see another salesman come into his territory.

Staffing policy in the sales organization is to expand the number of employees only when the prospective market can support their expenses.

The production organization prefers to be looked on as too lean rather than too fat. The sales organization prefers

36

having too many customers to having too many salesmen.

These attitudes contrast directly with those in most staff and support functions. If both the president and executive vice president want to consult a lawyer at the same time, the legal department feels it essential to have a lawyer available for each. In fact, the legal department will consider it essential to have two lawyers available *in case* the president and executive vice president should each want to consult a lawyer at the same time.

In other words, many of those responsible for staff and support functions feel it essential to be staffed to handle the maximum load they can anticipate, even though such load would be abnormal. Managers of such functions expect to receive more criticism for not handling promptly all demands placed on them than they do for increasing their expenses. Consequently, normal overhead staffing policy is to have adequate personnel not to handle average minimum load but to cover maximum peak load.

This attitude toward overhead staffing is grounded at least partially in the fundamentally dispensable character of overhead functions. The president does not have to consult a lawyer or have legal opinion if he does not want to. People in staff positions react, at least subconsciously, to the inherently tenuous nature of their positions by trying to build indispensability into their positions. The lawyer will always be ready to counsel the president whenever he is called on so that he will stand a better chance of being called on in the future. He may seek to supply not only legal advice when asked for it but also general business counsel as opportunities may offer. In any case, the staffing policy in overhead functions will be in the direction of being able to supply all requests for advice, information, or service on demand.

Because this policy inevitably leads to overstaffing for the normal average load, it results in a situation where there is actually insufficient utilization of overhead functions at any given time under usual conditions. Employees who have not enough work, however, are dissatisfied with such a condition. If they have any initiative at all, they will establish an appearance of busyness, and they will create things to do which seem to them to be useful. They will add depth to studies and analyses, broaden the scope of investigations, create new reports and new forms for collecting data periodically.

To the extent that such work as they have created proves, indeed, to be useful and used by other departments, they will devote concentrated effort to such activity. Once the activity is established, they will seek ways of improving and elaborating on it. This, in turn, will lead to the justification of additional staffing.

The charge of empire building, so often directed at overhead departments, is based on these two tendencies; that is, the psychological reaction to the dispensable nature of staff functions, and the tendency to manufacture work. The effect of both is expansionist.

As those in overhead functions anticipate or see a need for information, advice, or service in areas outside those of their basic charters, they seek to supply them. In most larger companies, you can find in overhead departments an accretion of functions that has been built up over the years around the central function for which they were created.

Likewise, as those in overhead areas manufacture work as a means of creating activity, you can find elaboration of their functions in depth. Much of the intense procedural activity that goes on in overhead departments is a result of this process. You can trace it in the number of forms generating data for overhead departments on aspects of production and sales, costs and expenses—which are converted, in turn, into statistical and analytical reports for manufacturing, sales, and management. As we will see again later, much of this activity has been taken over from the line organization as overhead departments developed more competence in, and capacity for, such procedural activity.

The result of this activity is to make overhead functions, in effect, indispensable to the rest of the organization. No company of any size nowadays could contemplate dispensing, for instance, with its accounting department. No one would be content to have the controller revert to book-keeping. Production supervisors cannot be expected to keep track of their own unit costs, and the president would have little confidence in mere oral reports of cost trends.

Furthermore, the competent specialists performing overhead functions are sure that the company could not operate without the services they are performing. In fact, they will be quick to point out that the company is really rather niggardly in supporting their functions. The president does not have enough background in their area of specialization to appreciate it properly and, unfortunately, the president neglected to consult them when he went ahead with that deal last week.

These accretive and elaborational tendencies in overhead functions are often encouraged by the attitude of managers toward them. "The service is there," a manager will say, "and the company is going to pay for it anyway, so we may as well use it." The implication is, of course, that "we" will use it because it is free, because it is there, and not because we really think we need it in this case.

Unfortunately, the executive in whom responsibility for overhead is centralized, whether at the executive or the profit-center level, is not aware of the extent to which an overhead function is used simply because it is there. When the time comes for annual budget review, the manager of that function will be able to point to the demands being placed on his department. He will not be aware of the fact that some of those demands were made only because "the company is already paying" for the function. When a higher level of overhead expenses is budgeted for next year (as seems to be almost inevitable), there will be no one who can point out that some of that increase is the result of overhead staffing policy.

Larger companies suffer a further deficiency in overhead staffing policy that smaller companies usually avoid. This deficiency might be called the sanctity of specialization. If you walk through the overhead departments of a large company, you are likely to find the clerks and secretaries in some departments overloaded while at the same time those in others have little to do. In a small company, by contrast, you will probably find a more uniform level of work—the president's secretary typing invoices, an office clerk helping out in the shipping department.

In a small office, people can be moved from one task to another as priorities shift; in a large company, organization of functional units seems to result in a psychological rigidity that prevents flow across organizational lines. There may be plenty of work that needs doing, but it is not, people are inclined to object, their type of work.

Take representatives from the same departments and put them together on a special task force or project team, however, and you will see they tend to work together on whatever needs doing to get the job done. Adherence to specialization becomes less important than their team objective.

On three counts, then, overhead staffing policy can contribute to excessive overhead costs. The sanctity of specialization inhibits evening out the workload. The desire to have capacity for the maximum load leads to general over-staffing. The desire to build indispensability into staff work leads to elaboration of procedural activity. These problems pose a challenge which is peculiar to modern business. It is not yet clear how it is best met.

Paying for Overhead

We look to the market to justify the products and services we sell. If there is enough demand, actual or potential, at a sufficient price to pay a suitable return on assets held for the shareholders, such demand provides the economic justification for the business we are in. A similar consideration should apply to all the items that make up controllable overhead expenses.

Unfortunately, it is often difficult to apply such considerations to them. As we have already seen, one factor that may contribute to the amount of overhead is usage, partly because a function is there and being paid for anyhow. Another may be the creation of an artificial demand for it—all divisions are instructed to use it. Obviously, there is a limit beyond which an enterprise can afford no more overhead. This fact, however, is true only of gross overhead; it can scarcely be applied to any individual item. Nevertheless, to control the total it is necessary, also, to control individual items.

There is no satisfactory way to define what overhead items are essential to a company, or how much of any one item is essential. Let anyone who doubts this unequivocal statement try to define the limits himself. Those in charge of overhead functions will gladly point out many areas in which there is, from their points of view, insufficient expenditure. Those in charge of profit centers to which a larger amount of overhead is allocated every year will be happy to tell you about examples, from their points of view, of frills, gold plating, and unnecessary services. Taking into account the criteria of optimization of profit and perpetuation of the company in the healthiest condition, how much, indeed, should a company pay for, say, internal audit, legal counsel, and computer services?

Obviously, there is no scientific answer to this question; any answer that is given will reflect the "style" of management. Under most circumstances, it is necessary to effect a compromise between the two points of view cited.

Since no answer is wholly right, a process of multiple decisions will usually provide the best solution. The marketplace provides such a process for products and services. The nearest equivalent that can be offered in respect to overhead within a company is this: The total cost of any item of controllable overhead must be authorized by, and charged to, the person "consuming" that item. If the manager of a profit center approves and pays for a service, the service is justified economically. If one manager buys much of a service and others do not, that service is questionable economically and that manager may need extra supervision. If the managers do not buy it, it is not justified economically. If the president authorizes an expense chargeable only to general overhead, he should have to consider the effect of that charge on profit and weigh its economic justification.

Four aspects of this principle need elaboration to appreciate its validity.

1. The person authorizing the expense must have a free choice to use or not to use the service and to buy it externally or internally. Furthermore, it must be very clear to subordinate managers that they have such a choice. They must understand that they do not have to buy it simply because someone from a staff department in the head office tells them it would be a good idea. In effect, the element of competition has to be introduced to make this principle effective. By this means, managers can apply the same methods of cost reduction in overhead areas that they use

in respect to their direct costs. Given the opportunity, managers will compete with each other in controlling overhead they are responsible for. The manager of one division will try to get the function performed at a cost lower than that of any other manager. The basic difficulty with allocation or proration of overhead is that there can be no real choice or competition between methods of performing overhead functions.

2. The person making the choice must be aware of the true cost to the company of the overhead item. Even where company policy permits a free choice, decisions may be biased because, for instance, the accounting system does not associate all costs with the item. Total cost of an overhead function includes: salaries, fringe benefits, rent, light, heat and power, telephone and telegraph, travel, depreciation, its own supervision and common facilities, and services from associated departments. It is because the true costs of an overhead function are usually not easily measured that services provided within a high-overhead company may appear to be less costly than those which can be purchased from outside sources with low overheads and salary structures. Common examples are contract maintenance and guard services. Unless there is evaluation of costs of services on a comparable basis, decisions made in regard to overhead functions will not really be free choices.

3. It is difficult in most companies to establish which one person is responsible for all the expenses charged to an overhead item. An advertising department, for instance, may serve a number of sales managers, handle institutional advertising for the company, prepare recruiting

material for the personnel department, and so on. Other departments may charge expenditures on pamphlets, general meetings, and reproduction services to the code for advertising unbeknownst to the advertising manager. In this, as in many respects, accounting practice is at variance with management principles. Obviously, in this example, there are many people responsible for many "advertisings." There can be no very effective control unless each "advertiser" authorizes, and is charged with, each of his expenditures so that he can be held accountable for the expenditures he has approved. The advertising manager may coordinate and monitor such expenditures, but he cannot really be held accountable for them. Furthermore, it is against all his best instincts to hold them down when he believes the company could use more advertising effectively.

No matter how essential it may be to account for advertising as a line item in overhead, it is impossible to establish real control of overhead unless responsibility for charges is unified and accountability is established. Responsibility must be fixed in the line organization where responsibility for profit is located. It cannot be placed in the staff organization because the staff cannot be held accountable. If, for example, as principal officer the president is named defendant in a suit, he can pass the blame, but not accountability, to his general counsel. In the same way, he can blame his advertising manager for increased expenses, but he must look to himself and his sales managers or managers of profit centers to fix responsibility for the situation.

45

Discharge of responsibility can be measured either by subcoding overhead accounts or by a subordinate system of memorandum accounting outside the official accounting system. Whatever the mechanism used, it must be designed to place charges and approvals on those who can have free control of them and can be held accountable for their actions.

4. If users of overhead functions approve and pay for them, a situation will arise in overhead departments similar to that in existing plants: There will be some unused capacity, intermittently or continually. There will be charges to "idle time," as it is called in respect to direct labor. It is just as important to measure unused capacity in overhead departments as it is to measure idle time in plants and calls-per-day of the sales force; each indicates the way a company is exploiting its manpower resources.

The amount and consistency of idle time in an overhead department will reveal the extent to which its activities are economically justified. This may indicate to management that provision of a service by a permanent internal organization is not warranted. Or this may indicate a change in emphasis as to the character of overhead function provided internally or procured externally; whether it should emphasize professional counseling, service, or analytical functions. The existence of excess capacity will force management to review the scope of overhead functions. There will be greater tendency to challenge them and better justification for expanding them.

There is always great resistance to a system of direct accounting for overhead areas. Some will resist it on the ground that it is demeaning to the professional character of their work. If they were in private practice, however, they would have to follow some system for relating time consumed to amount charged. Furthermore, their charges would have to include an overhead rate that would absorb idle time. Others will object that their time cannot be divided accurately among their various activities. The same people, on the other hand, must furnish currently a formula for allocating their expenses. For anyone who does not keep records of time spent by charge codes, the thought of adopting this practice is distasteful. Nevertheless, such records can be kept, they can be approximately correct, and they can serve the intended purpose.

Another major area of resistance to a change in method of charging overhead can be expected from accounting. It appears easier to charge to a code representing function than to an area of responsibility. It appears easier to allocate general overhead on a set formula than to split it up on the basis of use. It is relatively complicated to add its own overhead to an overhead function with strict accounting accuracy and to roll those charges around to various departments.

Furthermore, the controller will argue, there is no improvement in accuracy over his present method of allocation. According to the checks he has made, his present degree of accuracy is within 1 or 2 percent of any method for direct-charging overhead. His method is much more efficient.

All these arguments, however, avoid the central issue. The objective is to control and inhibit the growth of overhead and to develop the same efficiency in the utilization of overhead functions as has been developed in the utilization of labor, materials, and plant. If overhead functions were all procured from outside, like materials, charges made for them would include the cost of accounting for them properly. There is a tendency to think they are cheaper, when supplied internally, because they are not accounted for as exactly as a supplier would account for them.

In order to accomplish control in the overhead area, line managers must be provided with certain tools so that they will have incentive and ability to exercise control. (As an indication of how one firm has controlled its overhead rate, see Exhibit 2.) Such tools have helped greatly in giving subordinate managers incentive to reduce direct costs, control selling expenses, and keep the cost of direct support functions in line. The necessary incentive has been provided, to a great extent, by decentralizing responsibility for profit making to subordinate profit centers and for unit costs to cost centers. It is easier not to do this; it is easier to keep accounting records for a company as a whole, avoiding the difficulty of transfers between profit centers, allocation of charges to profit centers, and maintenance of *pro forma* balance sheets and profit and loss reports by profit centers. In spite of difficulties and even controversies as to methodology, modern accounting provides the means for accomplishing this management objective.

In the same way, modern accounting, particularly with the advent of computers, can provide the instrumentality for overhead control. And the essence of control is to unify

responsibility for elements of expense, establish accountability, and provide incentive for efficient utilization of
controllable items of overhead.

EXHIBIT 2

OVERHEAD COSTS
E. I. du Pont de Nemours & Co., Inc.

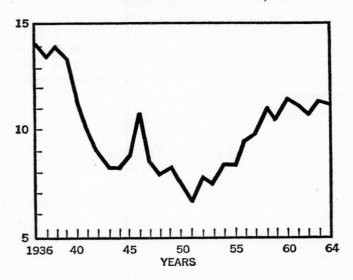

*Selling, general, and administrative expenses as
percent of sales.*

Du Pont uses a system by which divisional profit centers
"pay for" overhead functions to the extent that they use
them.

From its high rate during the depression, Du Pont's overhead as a percentage of sales dropped to a low during

World War II, dropped further during the Korean conflict. It has been held under its prewar rate ever since.

This company is noted, of course, for its effective management of a large and complex enterprise. The curve of its overhead rate indicates one way in which its reputation has been earned. Readers can compare the records of their own companies by plotting their own selling, general, and administrative rates on this chart. It would be accidental if the level of rates were to correspond directly because of differences between companies in the classification of accounts as well as the varying requirements of different businesses. Nevertheless, comparison of trends in rates can be made directly. And it is in the trend of its rates that a company can demonstrate its proficiency in the utilization of overhead functions.

Essentiality of Overhead Functions

In addition to establishing accountability for overhead expenses, management can investigate the essentiality of overhead functions being performed. For purposes of analysis, these functions can be divided into three categories: counseling, services, and procedural activity. It is not necessary to define these classifications accurately for this discussion, nor is it necessary to decide whether a particular activity should be considered as falling exactly under one or the other.

Counseling, in general, relates to the professional aspects of overhead functions. Managers at all levels have the need to call on staff for advice, information, and guidance in appropriate areas of specialization. The essentiality of such counsel is best established by means of economic justification. If a manager thinks it worth paying for counsel, it can be considered justified. If he feels that he will not receive enough value from it to pay for it, it is probably not justified.

It is true that some people run to doctors and lawyers at the least excuse. It is true, also, that some managers develop the habit of consulting particular staff members on every problem they encounter, whether or not it is within their fields of special competence.

A more important tendency to correct, however, is the desire of staff specialists to be in on everything, to be party to every decision, to sit on every committee and attend every meeting. Both tendencies can be minimized if managers have to pay the charges.

There is no other way of measuring the essentiality of counseling. There is no standard to measure by; hence the use of economic justification. You may criticize a manager's judgment, after the fact, for not having consulted a particular staff specialist on some matter. Lacking stated company policy that he must consult that specialist on that matter, you can only call into question the manager's ability to exercise responsibility delegated to him; he has used his judgment, and events have proved that he used it poorly.

If there is a stated company policy which leaves subordinate managers no option in consulting specialists, then they cannot control that part of overhead and the charges should not be placed on them. In such case the point of control is the source of the policy, and the charge should be placed on the executive if that is where the policy was established.

To the extent that the company does not feel safe in delegating to subordinate managers authority to follow their own judgment in this area, it can follow either of two courses: (1) restrict delegation by policy statements or (2) designate staff specialists to audit the performance of subordinate units. The latter approach is certainly preferred if one of the objectives of the company is to develop strong line managers.

Although internal auditing has been used for years in the financial aspects of management, equivalent means are applied insufficiently in other areas. It can be used as well, for instance, to monitor compliance with the Sherman Act, or the effectiveness of local purchasing, or the entertainment expenses of salesmen.

Post facto review has these advantages:

1. It does not impede current actions of the line organization.
2. By reporting back through the line, it strengthens the line and its authority over subordinate units.
3. It enables managers to reappraise their own performance, train their subordinates better, and broaden their area of competency.
4. It reduces the future need for counseling in that area: As managers develop their own competency, it is gradually self-liquidating (an ideal eagerly to be sought for in overhead areas!).

Auditing, as a service, and counseling in many areas are

performed for the company as a whole at the request of executives and, to a degree, on the initiative of staff members. Just as manufacturing generates its own overhead expenses in production support areas, so too does the executive department. It has its own staff and draws on the overhead departments. Among other things, it may require them to audit performance in subordinate units. Indeed, the National Industrial Conference Board has noted a trend in larger corporations to the creation of small, highly professional super-staff departments for the purpose of serving executive echelons exclusively.

At the executive level especially, the relationship between staff and line is intimate. It is difficult to curb rising expenditures, and there is a great tendency to rationalize any expense on the ground that if people want it they should have it.

Again, the best corrective is that the charge system make clear to the executive the effect on profit of charges attributable to him. It is rather important that counseling services and reporting to the executive be clearly differentiated from charges laid on subordinate managers because of requirements in company policy. Under some circumstances, at least, it may be desirable for the executive to challenge the amount and essentiality of expenses in both categories. This is extremely difficult to do if distinctions are not drawn on the basis of accountability for the different classes of overhead. Furthermore, historical data are as necessary in overhead control as in cost control, and the system should provide for both.

Services are overhead activities which are authorized

by, are performed for, and should be charged to the executive, subordinate managers, or another overhead department. Examples are preparing plans and specifications for a new plant, conducting an advertising campaign, performing a study of overhead expenses.

In this category of activities, essentiality of the service is established when it is authorized. Before the assignment is made, it is decided that this activity should be carried out. Normally the decision is made by the person who will be charged with the expense, and normally the same person is accountable for the results. Needless to say, the system should charge him with the total cost of the work he authorizes. In general, however, this type of activity does not require a determination of essentiality, other than that made on a case-by-case basis by those who are responsible for their decisions and are supposed to live within their budgets.

The problem for management in regard to overhead services lies in the procedures surrounding them. Authorization, for instance, is seldom as simple a procedure as has been outlined. Frequently, a set of papers may have to cross a dozen different desks before all the signatures, initials, and comments have been collected that are required by established practice or written management procedures. Much of this paper passing really represents an evasion of responsibility. The theory seems to be that, if a dozen people signify approval, no one person will have to carry the blame. Some of it also represents people checking other people in the hope of picking up any error before an expenditure is made.

It is important that the procedure for authorization of services be quite clear in delineating responsibility, whether the services are obtained from within or without. What a man authorizes and the way he authorizes it tell a great deal about his potential to discharge greater responsibility. The only safeguard needed is that his superior approve the cost of the services he authorizes. Any further checks on the services will prevent a clear definition of accountability as well as the comparison of costs to results.

The final category of overhead functions is *procedural activity*. By this is meant all the flow of information and forms, all the collecting and reporting of data that cross organizational lines—the true cost of which no one knows, let alone controls. This type of expense encompasses all the routine, largely nonprofessional clerical and statistical activities of the company. For example, data on various activities are required to be generated, compiled, and reported by those who are supposedly responsible for those activities. This information is passed up the organizational ladder—to the production manager, for instance. Upon recompiling, consolidating, and analyzing the information, he prepares summary and detailed reports for use by others in the company. Included in this category are such things as:

- Engineering drawings, specifications, construction, real property records.
- Purchasing, receiving, payment, and inventory procedures.
- Sales orders, warehousing, shipping, billing, collecting, sales statistics.

55

- Time card, payroll, cost reports, production statistics.

If you analyze established procedures, you may come across such anomalies as these:

1. A manager charged with the responsibility of managing a $10 million annual payroll efficiently is not authorized to make overhead expenditures of more than $1,000.

2. It costs a company $30 each to double-check a class of expenditures ranging up to $1,000. There are 150 such items a year. Normal error does not exceed 10 percent, plus or minus, once in 25 times, and the probability of 100 percent error is nil.

Obviously the problem is to analyze the essentiality of the procedures followed and, in some cases, to evaluate the relationship between cost and potential liability or loss. In approaching the problem, there are a number of questions to be answered:

- What is the existing procedure?
- What steps in this procedure cannot be dispensed with under any circumstances?
- To whom is authority delegated to approve the expense?
- Is the same person accountable for costs and results?
- Does he have the right to buy internally or externally?
- Does the system give him the total cost of providing the service internally?

- Does the delegation to him stipulate that he obtain the concurrence of other overhead functions?
- Is the delegation to him in the form of an aggregate budget, a line item in a budget, or a separate line item?
- To whom must total cost and results be reported for record purposes?
- Who should review the results as a measure of (1) managerial performance and (2) efficiency in performing the overhead function involved?

To get at the answers to these questions, it is best to develop a flow chart of the particular procedure involved in all its ramifications. It is then possible to strip it to its essentials. Probably, they will be: source of authority, point of approval, point of performance, point of review, places of records.

As the questions indicate, there must be clarity in delegation if procedures are to be simplified. Too often, double-checking and concurrences are built into procedures because authority is not properly delineated. In such cases, costs are added because responsibility is not unified. The best way to minimize mistakes, after all, is to have it clear who is at fault when a mistake is made.

It is important, when plotting the flow of a procedure, to chart all related flow. You may well find, then, that a single procedure requires repetition of the same flow two to four times to accomplish a single result. It is quite common that both budgetary approval and later item approval are required for a single expenditure. You may find, also, that the same procedural flow is repeated on a purchase requisition, a purchase order, a receival notice, and a payment voucher—all for the same item. If so, you should be grateful that your production line does not copy your practice in performing overhead functions!

These, of course, are the areas where bureaucracy flourishes and red tape encumbers line action. These are the areas where activity can be measured only by degree of busyness because any measurement of results—number of drawings made per draftsman, number of purchase orders placed per buyer, number of sales orders processed per clerk—is essentially meaningless. However, these are normally the indices used by managers of overhead departments to show progress.

The conventional approach to cost improvement in this area is to speed up processing of forms and data. More money is invested in faster machines and communications. More procedures are automated. Calculations are transferred to computers and standing matter is reproduced by machine. Those responsible for processing the data devise new forms on which data are required to be supplied to them because the new forms will enable them to process more data faster, more completely. As a result, new forms become more complex and reports become bulkier.

Under usual concepts of organization this is the only practical approach. Those in charge of the function—for example, engineering, purchasing, accounting—control only part of the procedures and only part of the costs involved. Normally they derive their data from others, and their reports are utilized by others. They supply an engine which does some or much of the procedural "work."

They consider that the speed and horsepower of that engine are their responsibility. What is required, however, is examination of the total procedure to see if that engine can be eliminated entirely:

- What are the elements of this procedure?
- How does the work flow?
- What are its essential elements?
- What alternate work flow could be devised to eliminate inessential steps?
- How well could the company function if the entire procedure were eliminated?

It should be noted that this approach can be taken only by someone above the functional overhead departments. Practically speaking, that means the executive. The amount of investigation required, however, makes it impractical for the executive to carry it out. Staff or outside help may well be needed.

Control of overhead requires determination of the essentiality of the counseling, services, and procedural activity performed. As far as practicable, the decision as to essentiality should be made by the manager of the line unit who will be charged with the cost and accountable for results.

Each of the three categories of overhead described requires a different approach. They are controllable in different ways at various organizational levels. For this reason, if for no other, a consistent philosophy has to be developed in the company, and it must be consistently applied. There is no other area, however, where management can more directly influence profitable performance.

PART II

A Program for Controlling Overhead

II

We have discussed a number of the phenomena that characterize the overhead problem in business. We have considered many of the steps that should be taken to insure adequate control of overhead. No businessman of experience would think, however, that there is anything easy about controlling overhead. There is a lot more to it than merely reading a book. It cannot be done by slapping the desk top and saying: "Let's put on a campaign!" It cannot be accomplished, either, by calling in a vice president and telling him to do it, while everyone else walks away from the problem.

In this section, we will take up in order the attitudes and actions that are necessary to have a successful program of overhead control.

Objectives of Overhead Control

The purposes of a program of overhead control are to limit expenses in overhead categories so as to improve profits and increase competitive strength, and to develop efficiencies in the performance of overhead functions similar to those that have been developed in manufacturing and sales.

It will be noted that the objectives are twofold: (1) to give management more margin for maneuvering between gross and net profit, and (2) to obtain greater efficiency in overhead functions. One factor in the gradual decline in profitability of manufacturing companies in recent years is a squeeze on net profit by overhead charges. To a marked degree, business has been able to offset higher labor and materials costs by operating efficiency. Costs are higher, of course, than they were in the past. But trends are better observed when expressed as a percentage of sales. Data are not available from which to generalize on the experience of business as a whole. The impression persists, however, that many companies show a favorable trend in manufacturing and selling costs when related to sales, but that the relation of overhead to sales has been less favorable in recent years.

There is certainly such a trend in companies which have experienced growth in volume and heavier investment in plant. For those companies, the cost of materials consumed per unit of output probably has not increased much (as can be seen in the wholesale price index). In fact, more efficient utilization of material, both from improved processing and from more efficient design of products, may well have reduced cost of materials as a percentage of unit of output. Likewise, power costs probably have been reduced. While labor rates have risen dramatically, they have been offset to a large extent by reduction in the labor content per unit of output through improved processing, automation, and product design.

Similarly, in selling, more effective use of advertising and packaging, improvements in distribution methods, and growth of markets in volume and density have improved marketing efficiency enough to compensate for the higher cost of salesmen and advertising space. This experience may derive to a large extent from the unified control and unified organizational responsibility for costs in these areas. Where similar experience obtains in the overhead area, it gives management greater flexibility in its options to increase payout, increase investment, or strengthen marketing. It is when management has room to make choices that it shows its creative ability.

Second, there is the objective of the efficient use of overhead. All theory indicates that overhead should decline with volume. Existing overhead groups should be able to perform their functions even though volume increases. No matter how much the company grows, there should still be only one president and the same number of receptionists as at present, and the load on accounting should not increase proportionately to volume.

Theory to the contrary, experience indicates that there is a law (especially applicable to general overhead) saying: Overhead expenses will increase at least as fast as sales. Obviously, there is a breakdown in management control when this happens. When volume increased in World War II and the Korean conflict, overhead rates dropped sharply. In the late fifties and early sixties, many companies experienced climbing overhead rates in spite of expanding sales. During World War II, there were constraints on the expansion of overhead imposed through government regulation. In recent times, there has been no such artificial situation: Companies have been free to add to overhead functions as they liked—and many have liked too much!

This condition has been masked to a degree in most industries by heightened competition and resulting pressures on prices. It is only revealed when the trends in the principal elements of costs are studied as they relate to volume and sales.

There are fashions in management, as in most things, and it is probable that managements have been too much beguiled by the remarkable development of specialized knowledge and the glitter of new technology in performance of overhead functions. Most new things in the general overhead area are studied only incrementally. Their proponents always seem to be able to justify them economically. It is only when you analyze the gross effect that you find your overhead rates have somehow gone up another notch.

An industrial company has to have labor and materials. In spite of the increased cost of these two basic elements, many companies have found ways to use them so much more effectively that manufacturing costs do not take any larger slice out of a sales dollar than they used to. One way or another, methods have to be found so that total overhead represents a similar improvement in the cost of performing overhead functions.

These, then, are the twofold objectives of overhead control. They are sufficiently important to demand continuing management attention, in spite of all the other things pressing in on executives and managers alike.

Executive Attitude Toward Overhead Control

Probably more than in any other important aspect of company operations, effectiveness of overhead control reflects the attitude and style of the principal executive.

Manufacturing people can be expected to do their jobs even though the president does not do much more than review their performance periodically. The selling organization will keep making sales even though the salesmen see him only when he addresses their annual get-together. (This is not, of course, to endorse such negligent treatment of either of these vital functions.) As soon as he turns his back on overhead, however, he can expect control to slip.

In a peculiar way, control of overhead is a responsibility of the principal executive. He can delegate—and no doubt has—responsibility over manufacturing to one executive, over sales to another, or both to division heads to redelegate. In such cases, these executives have responsibility for, authority over, and accountability for the areas delegated to them. That delegation, hopefully, will include control over their own supporting general functions and considerable freedom as to where they obtain them.

But who is responsible, in like manner and to equivalent degree, over general overhead? The answer, evidently, is only the principal executive. He can delegate his responsibility in this respect only if he creates what is called in military organization a chief of staff—a person responsible for, and superior to, the heads of all overhead departments and overhead staff. In this case, the attitude we speak of will be that of the executive in such a position.

It is noteworthy that attitude is not a problem in controlling overhead in smaller companies. When a company is small enough that any increase in overhead will show up in next month's profit and loss statement, overhead control is an imperative for the principal executive. He has learned from experience that he must give unremitting attention to the level of overhead expenses. He has found that he has to relate any contemplated expense to total overhead rate. He knows that he can incur a new expense safely only when he can show a compensating saving which will be reflected in a lowered rate. As a consequence, he is likely to maintain a consistent attitude toward overhead expenses. His subordinates will be aware of his attitude and will govern themselves accordingly.

A similar attitude toward their own controllable overheads is usual among managers of decentralized cost and profit centers. They will point out that they are better in controlling their overheads than their parent organizations are in controlling their own. Apparently, somewhat the same forces shape the attitudes of those responsible in both cases. They are both constrained by profit performance in their current operating statements to maintain close control over their indirect costs. As a result they develop a disciplined approach toward overhead expenses.

In a large company there is no such immediate and direct connection between any particular item of overhead and the amount of profit, especially in respect to general overhead. The overhead totals that appear every month on operating statements are aggregates of many overhead items. Many different persons are "responsible" for them.

It is usually difficult to connect an authorization to spend with an increase in expenses. The increase may follow the authorization by months or even years. When you seek to learn the reason for an increase in a category of expense, you may be told: "The president approved that three months ago." It is difficult, and somewhat immaterial at the later date, to try to find out whether the increase had been properly projected and evaluated. Probably—for such is the nature of many of these expenses—it would be almost impossible to undo the authorization and have expenses revert to their former level.

Even the fact of increased expenses may be masked. A higher level of sales may seem to indicate that the current rate of expenses is "safe," even though the amount being spent on overhead is higher than ever. Accordingly, everyone relaxes, although the actual increase in overhead may be more than any possible gain from improvement in productive efficiency.

Another masking effect may be in the form of the profit

and loss statements themselves. These reports are designed to account for expenses rather than to control them. It is often difficult to ascertain trends in the flow of charges, adjustments, cross entries, and accruals.

For all these reasons, managerial attitude is crucial in controlling overhead. A correct attitude is forced on managers of smaller companies by the immediate relationship between expense and profit. A similar attitude appears most commonly in larger companies, under the pressures of depressed conditions. Otherwise, it can come about only as a matter of self-discipline on the part of the principal executive which he, in turn, imposes on the rest of management.

Control, of course, implies discipline. In business, it is a function of management to establish appropriate control. It is assumed that management will automatically exert appropriate financial controls, control of production costs, and so on. Proper management in the area of overhead expenses also requires control and an attitude as consistent as management applies to production costs and financial controls. This attitude will not come about by accident and will be largely ineffective if it is not held to consistently. It must derive from the top and receive expression from the principal executive. It is because there is a lack of consistent executive attitude toward overhead control that so many companies go through periodic crises to get overhead back in line. Surely it is better to keep it in line than to let it get out of hand. Whichever course is followed will be the one laid down by the principal executive.

A Program

Planning Overhead Control

Like every activity through which management expresses itself positively in the organization, overhead control involves planning. The principal executive cannot merely be a nay-sayer to every proposal for overhead spending any more than he can afford to reject every recommendation on plant investment. Utilization of gross profit, like that of cash flow, is an opportunity for management to make a direct contribution to the company.

Conversely, the principal executive cannot delegate management of overhead control to a staff statistician, accountant, or administrative assistant. The result might be good planning methodology, but it would be poor control. Preparation of plans for controlling overhead can be delegated; responsibility for planning cannot be. The proof is demonstrated when overhead gets out of hand and a president must account to his board of directors for lack of profits. The principal executive therefore owes it to himself to see that planning for overhead control is properly discharged.

The functions of planning, control, and supervision of overhead can be delegated, in fact, only to a level superior to the overhead functions themselves. As discussed earlier, such delegation involves the chief of staff concept. While common in military doctrine, it is unusual (but not unprecedented) in business to have a vice president in charge of overhead functions with actual authority over their expenses. This position, it should be noted, is different from that of the executive vice president, who is superior, under the president, to all line and staff functions.

The position of vice president for staff is in any case a difficult one; it is virtually untenable unless it receives the full support of the principal executive. It is in the area of overhead functions that tendencies toward empire building are most pronounced. Because of the specialized nature of those functions, it is not possible to have expertise in all of them. It requires careful judgment to avoid favoring some as against others.

The highly professional character of those in the upper echelons of overhead functions can lead to bypassing of the vice president for staff. Cliques can develop in the executive level to support one or another of the overhead groups in the treatment they receive at budget time.

These difficulties, however, are inherent in the problem of controlling overhead. If it were easily solved through a form of organization, it would no longer exist. How successful the principal executive is in delegating this problem to a vice president for staff will be a reflection of his own attitude and his ability to pick the right man.

Whether by the principal executive himself or by a vice president for staff acting for him, the overhead planning function must be discharged. In a large company, this function will itself require special staff work. It is not to be expected that the executive responsible will be able to carry out by himself the preparation of projections and budgets, analyses of performance, and reorganizations of procedures The number of staff necessary will vary between companies, depending on the amount of detail involved. The purpose of staff, in any case, is to develop information needed for planning and control, not to perform the planning function itself.

Economic projections. Because of the relationship between overhead rate and sales, overhead planning is based on the most likely projection of future business. Because of the fallibility of such projections, however, it must also take into account optimistic and pessimistic projections. These projections should forecast sales and direct costs.

In preparing overhead projections, the point of departure is the relationship between current expenses and current level of business. From this point it is necessary to project the incremental additions to expenses necessary to serve higher levels of business.

A word of caution needs to be inserted here: The fact that a particular category of overhead currently represents a certain ratio to sales does not indicate that it should represent the same ratio at other levels of sales. For many years now, it is true, the overhead policies of most companies have been saved by a nearly continuous growth curve. There is no assurance, however, that growth will always persist. It is no policy to say that we will always dedicate a set percentage of sales to support of overhead functions in the aggregate or to any one singly.

What needs to be determined, then, is what has to be committed to overhead expense. If such a level of expense leaves a balance, the first objective of overhead control will have been met: The company will have the option as to where that balance should be applied.

The pessimistic projection will give the basis for a plan of action if, in fact, the most likely forecast is not to be met. An appropriate fall-back plan will indicate areas where action can be taken and to what extent profitability can be preserved under adverse conditions.

Overhead projections should be built up from individual functions and items of expense to arrive at a total. This may well be the opposite approach to that taken in projecting sales. In the latter case, the approach may be based on the trend in gross national product and company share of the market. Use of such trends in overhead projections merely solidifies a ratio of overhead to sales and destroys the possibility of more efficient performance of overhead functions.

From this build-up, the planned level of expenses is established. The final plan, of course, will be a figure of total expense for the period which will incorporate executive judgment as to the requirements of the company and the most useful applications of gross profit.

Overhead budgets. The planned level of expenses must be converted into budgets. These can be regarded as quantitative expressions of the executive plan for overhead expenses. They are required for purposes of—

- Delegating authority to incur types of expenses to overhead departments.
- Monitoring actual amount and rate of expenditures against the plan.
- Making adjustments in the planned rate of expenditures to meet unforeseen circumstances.
- Supervising performance in overhead areas.

These budgets probably will be in a form different from present accounting reports. Normally, overhead expenses are attributed to functions (such as advertising) or to certain types of expenditures (such as state taxes). Neither of these examples is appropriate for overhead control: Many people contribute to advertising expenses, and state taxes are not subject to internal organization control. Obviously you need to project and account for state taxes as a part of total overhead. Likewise, it is important to know that the company is spending 10 percent more on advertising this year than last. Neither fact by itself is of much help in controlling overhead. Control, it is hardly necessary to point out, must be exerted through people in the organization; hence the importance of relating cost to *de facto* accountability.

In developing the format of budgets and internal overhead control reports, certain principles should be followed. Budgets and reports should be made to the level at which responsibility can be unified for the costs involved. In some cases, as we shall see later in considering reorganization of procedures, it is not possible to unify responsibility at any level for all the costs of a procedure. In these cases, expenses that can be determined should be adequately identified so that they can be monitored.

In general, there is better control of overhead when it is supervised at the lowest organizational level at which responsibility can be established. This is the reason for making charges out from overhead departments down to the level of cost centers. The general principle is to charge expenses where, in the organization, the service is used.

The person charged must then justify to himself and to his superior the costs he has incurred.

Similar considerations apply in making charges for services to the executive. Without such a system, over-zealous staff people or those anxious to ingratiate themselves at the highest level incur expenses for services that are not really wanted. In the same way, it is desirable to clarify executive responsibility for companywide expenses, which have a distressing tendency to grow even under an adequate system of budgeting, authorization, and accounting.

Whenever and wherever possible, budgets should be supplemented with projections of specific accomplishments or results. These should be milestones that can be placed on a Gantt chart; for example, conversion of records to tapes, development of a product. They should not be a mere measurement of activity. Such milestones give the supervising executive an objective measurement of performance which he can use to evaluate managers even though he knows nothing of computers or research and development.

In establishing overhead budgets, the executive has a choice between budgeting on plan or under plan. The method selected will demand a degree of confidence in the validity of projections, soundness of the back-off plan, and, finally, management philosophy. Certainly it is desirable to give overhead departments latitude to make preliminary studies of possible new activities and to have them know that budgets can be reopened for due cause. It seems advisable to have sufficient room provided for such normal adjustments that the plan itself does not have to be modified, except for a major change in conditions.

Management has the further problem, when determining overhead budgets, of avoiding favoring the "loud squawkers." This is an aspect of management in which only experience is an adequate guide. A system of overhead control, keying expenses to results as far as possible, will mitigate the problem without removing it.

These considerations have been applied to the outline of a format for overhead budget and expense reports in Exhibit 3. When appropriately detailed for the requirements of individual companies, a similar format will provide adequate information to convey the overhead plan to those responsible for carrying it out and to measure their performance. It is therefore an essential element in controlling overhead. Without it, adequate control and consistent policy are not to be expected.

EXHIBIT 3

OUTLINE OF FORMAT FOR BUDGET AND EXPENSE REPORTS

I. *Company and Executive Expenses*
1. Company noncontrollable (e.g., franchise tax)
2. Company general overhead
   a. Companywide expenses controllable by executive (e.g., donations, company picnic, industrial advertising)
   b. Expenses of overhead departments allocated to general overhead (see item II-2*e*)
3. Executive expenses
   a. Salaries and benefits
   b. Travel and entertainment
   c. Communications

   d. Other expenditures (e.g., books for executive use)

   e. Rent, light, heat

   f. Depreciation

   g. Charges from overhead departments for counseling, auditing, and services

  4. Executive, direct staff (e.g., secretarial, personal assistants, detailed as under item 3)

  5. Amount allocable to profit centers, items 1–4

 II. *Overhead Department Expenses*

  1. Department noncontrollable (if any)

  2. Department overhead

   a. Supervision and secretarial, rent, general expenditures, depreciation

   b. Charges from other departments to department overhead (e.g., cost of recruiting new employees for this department)

   c. Idle time of personnel and services otherwise charged out direct

   d. Services not charged out direct (e.g., interoffice messenger service administered by this department)

   e. Total general overhead (sum of items 1 and 2) charged to company general overhead (item I-2*b*)

  3. Department direct services

   a. Charges from other departments to department direct services (e.g., reproduction costs incurred by this department for a booklet prepared for a profit center)

   b. Expenses for counseling and services charged direct to other departments, the executive, profit or cost centers.

  4. Total charged to other departments

  5. Total cost of this function, items 2*e* plus 4

 III. *Profit Center* (e.g., divisional) *and Cost Center* (e.g., production department) *Overhead*

  1. Noncontrollable overhead of center

2. Allocated share of company and executive expenses (if profit is computed at divisional level)
3. Controllable overhead
   a. Supervision, cost of direct support, its other charges to its own overhead
   b. Charges from overhead departments for counseling and services
4. Total overhead of center

It is to be anticipated that there will be internal resistance to this element of control within the company. Overhead departments will object to more detailed accounting for their expenses than they now provide. Accounting will resist a system which adds overhead to overhead and rolls one set of overhead charges to another before charging or allocating them out. Even some executives may object to a more careful delineation of responsibility for general overhead.

These difficulties are, essentially, those that appear when initiating any broad change. Once accounting has adapted to the new procedure, it will operate with no more than the usual daily problems attendant on accounting for costs. In a few months overhead departments will code charges as a matter of course. You will be looking, in any case, only for the degree of approximate accuracy that will enable you to plan and carry out overhead control. In order to plan you will have to organize staff for a flow of information to project future overhead expenses. You will need to plan a rate of expense that will best meet your conception of the requirements of your company. You will have to get that plan converted into budgets by which you can measure progress down the road. You will have to monitor performance by every firm measurement you can find. The fact that you do these things, however, will make it known to the organization that you expect results and more effective performance. And employees will always try to deliver what the boss wants.

Reorganization of Procedures

Reduction of overhead means change. Except for a basic reorganization of the company, nowhere is this more important than in procedural activity. Change here means simplification; elimination of steps which do not help produce or sell. It means, also, elimination of duplication, retention of records, parallel dissemination of information. It requires mobilization of regular staff and special study teams to take a fresh look at the performance of overhead functions.

With executive responsibility for overhead established, more positive steps can be taken to improve the effective utilization of overhead. The most important expense area not covered so far relates to the routine paperwork that encumbers every company. There are two important milestones to emulate in controlling the cost of procedural activity. The first of these was the decision by Sears, Roebuck and Co. to abandon the retention of consumer mail orders. In its earlier procedure, Sears used to retain customer orders along with its forms acknowledging and confirming shipment. This system, as you can imagine, required aisles of files and a host of clerks to work them.

Now Sears returns customer correspondence and shipping forms when the order is filled. Claims are settled on an ad hoc basis. The reduction in cost of procedural activity more than offsets the adjustments Sears must make. Since fighting customers' claims does nothing to increase profits, Sears has come out a net gainer.

The second of these milestones was Kaiser Aluminum & Chemical Corporation's decision to send out blank checks for vendors to complete on all purchases of less than $1,000. In Kaiser's cash order system, a blank check goes out with the purchase order. The vendor makes the shipment, then completes and deposits the check. Kaiser is saved the procedural activity of matching the order to shipping papers, to the invoice, and to accounts payable.

Those two milestones are marks of the objectives to strive for in evaluating paperwork routine.

Part of the cost of procedural activity will appear in budget and expense reports—as, for example, in Exhibit 3, item II-2*d,* "services not charged out direct." Like an iceberg, however, much of the cost of routine procedures is not visible. In fact, total cost can merely be approximated at best.

To appreciate both the problem and the approach to a solution, it is necessary to go into detail. Since procedures vary so between companies, a hypothetical case will be used. Exhibit 4 is a flow chart of the paperwork routine a company may go through in making a sale. From the time that a salesman takes an order until payment is received, paper flows through one organizational unit after another. Many different entities need to know things about

EXHIBIT 4

PAPERWORK STEPS IN MAKING A SALE

 1 Salesman writes order.

2 Local sales office checks and transmits order.

3 Sales department checks order, posts order book and transmits order.

 4 Credit department checks customer credit, notes order on trade record and transmits order.

 5 Accounting department checks arithmetic, posts backlog, sends copy to billing department, transmits order.

 6 Billing department files copy in suspense.

7 Sales department acknowledges order and transmits.

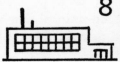 **8** Distribution point checks order, prepares item for shipment, prepares packing slip, notifies traffic department.

9 Traffic department selects carrier, schedules pick-up, prepares bill of lading.

10 Distribution point ships to customer, notifies sales department, sales office, billing department.

11 Billing department invoices customer, notifies sales department, collections, credit, accounts receivable.

12 Sales department posts order book.

13 Accounting department receives payment, notifies sales, collections, credit, accounts receivable.

14 Sales department notifies salesman who goes after next order.

the transaction in the course of its consummation. (No attempt has been made to trace the flow of information after the transaction has been completed and it becomes a part of company statistics in financial, production, and marketing reports.)

Of the 14 paperwork steps shown in Exhibit 4, only six (numbers 4–6, 9, 11, 13) would be accounted for under "services not charged out direct" in budget and expense reports (Exhibit 3, item II-2d). The costs of six other steps (numbers 1–3, 7, 12, 14) would be buried in selling expense, while the remaining steps (numbers 8, 10) would be hidden in manufacturing support. Nevertheless, you can approximate the total cost of this iceberg by taking the monthly salaries of all employees working on it and adding an overhead rate appropriate for your company. The result will probably be a noticeable percentage of net sales for the month.

No matter how hard you search you will not be able to find the inventor of this procedure. It just grew. It has to go through each group because it involves each area of interest. As to who designed it, who is responsible for it, who controls it—no one! Yet the whole procedure has to exist just to put through the paperwork in order to make a sale.

To the executive responsible for overhead, such a situation is a challenge. Any costs saved in such a procedure are a direct addition to profit. Savings made will not reduce one whit the company's ability to manufacture or sell its products. In fact, cost savings should result, also, in time savings and better customer services.

A Program

The executive can disregard the specific interests of individual organizational elements and analyze such a procedure from the point of view of functional essentiality. In this case, what are the indispensable elements in the transaction? There has to be an order from the customer. There has to be a shipment to the customer. There has to be an invoice and bill of lading sent to the customer. Payment has to be received from the customer. That receipt has to be entered in the official accounts. If necessary, the company could dispense with all other paperwork steps in making a sale. Do you doubt that statement? Then examine each step and see what the company would lose if a step were eliminated.

> Step 1: Salesman writes order. Is essential. There has to be an order from the customer.
>
> Step 2: Local sales office checks and transmits order. The order must be transmitted from the field to the factory or warehouse from which delivery is made.[1]
>
> Step 3: Sales department checks order, posts order book, and transmits order. Can be eliminated. The salesman will not make the mistake twice of ordering gadgets when the customer wants widgets; he will have to placate his customer and sell the gadg-

[1] In many businesses, Steps 1 and 2 are combined because the customer sends a purchase order to the local sales office. Some companies have educated customers to send orders direct to plants or distribution centers. "Automatic ordering" is a further possibility, tying customers' computers to those of suppliers. Bypassing the sales office, however, puts the seller at the mercy of the buyer, and most companies will resist these trends in order to retain better control of their own destinies.

ets too. The sales manager has never yet made a decision based on information in the order book.

Step 4: Credit department checks customer credit, notes order on trade record, and transmits order. Can be eliminated. Put the onus on the local sales offices to call the credit department when there is doubt about credit. Most sales are to existing customers on whom there are records of payment. How much do you want to invest in procedural double-checking to avoid a possible loss?

Step 5: Accounting department checks arithmetic, posts backlog, sends copy to billing department, transmits order. Can be eliminated. Clerks in the sales offices can multiply and add as well as clerks in accounting. The president looks only at a dollar total for backlog (if he checks this at all), and the sales offices can add up the total of open orders in five minutes.

Step 6: Billing department files copy in suspense. Why do it? Billing clerk has to file copy of order, match shipping notice to it, prepare and mail out bill (see Step 11).

Step 7: Sales department acknowledges order and transmits. Can be eliminated. Local sales office can type acknowledgment of order and a copy providing instructions to distribution point.

Step 8: Distribution point checks order, prepares item for shipment, prepares packing slip, notifies traffic department. It is essential to prepare for shipment to customer.

Step 9: Traffic department selects carrier, schedules pick-up, prepares bill of lading. Can be eliminated, except when customer has not specified carrier and when routing is not known at distribution point. In these cases, traffic can be called for advice.

Step 10: Distribution point ships to customer, notifies sales department, sales office, billing department. Can be combined with Step 8. Distribution point can type manifold form to provide bill of lading, packing slip, shipping notice to customer and local sales office.

Step 11: Billing department invoices customer, notifies sales department, collections, credit, accounts receivable. Can be eliminated. Local sales office can type invoice as part of manifold form when it types acknowledgment of order. It can mail invoice when it receives notice from Step 10. It can give accounts receivable daily total of unpaid invoices.

Step 12: Sales department posts order book. Can be eliminated when you eliminate order book.

Step 13: Accounting department receives payment, notifies sales, collections, credit, accounts receivable. Local sales office can collect payment, send daily payment record to accounting and sales departments.

Step 14: Sales department notifies salesman who goes after next order. Can be eliminated. Salesman has already gone after next order.

Before any attempt is made to rationalize this change in procedure, a number of observations can be made about the 14-step routine. It puts the maximum amount of impedance on the completion of the action that started with the customer's order. Every step that is taken involves delay, postponing the time when money is collected. It is almost inevitable that one piece of paper will get mislaid or misrouted. And when this happens, the result will be an endless amount of double-checking, searching, telephone calls, and apologizing to the customer.

The system is sure to result in errors. Every time something has to be copied or posted, there is a potential for discrepancy. This type of error is the most difficult to correct because it means a complete breakdown in the routine of posting and filing until such time as discrepant information is reconciled by verification of source data.

The entire procedure is as if it were designed to prevent the location of responsibility. Everyone in the chain can point the finger of blame to someone else. Even the salesman who started it all can turn on those pointing at him by saying: "You are supposed to check that; you have the records on that."

With this kind of procedure, specialists are so busy with the routine that they do not have time to use their expertise. It is an abasement of their training to overwhelm them with record keeping and checking of forms. This they are prone to do to themselves because, among other reasons, accomplishment is more apparent in a report of number of orders processed than in studying a means of reducing overhead. While busyness may be a safe refuge for specialists, it is not the occupation management is generally seeking when it selects them.

When analyzing this procedure, the responsible executive should attempt to design an idealized method which, as far as possible, will minimize the number of steps, unify responsibility, and utilize specialists as such. A procedure such as this has initiating and completing actions; in this case:

customer's order ⟶ delivery of product

invoice ⟶ payment.

Ancillary actions should be accomplished as a part of these essential actions. They should, however, be performed— if at all—only to the extent that they contribute to the essential actions. Once started, there is a tendency for ancillary actions to become an end in themselves. The only reason for performing them lies in the extent to which they support or reduce the cost of essential actions.

In many cases, these considerations will result in performance of essential actions on a decentralized basis, rather than gathering information from the source, processing it on high-speed equipment, and returning it for the completing action. You may have to remind yourself that there is cost involved in preparing information to be gathered from the field in a form suitable for processing on computers. If the procedure is properly designed, the cost of the routine of gathering, processing, and returning may be mostly or entirely redundant. That is the case in the present example. Exhibit 5 charts a revised procedure for making a sale. It illustrates how the considerations we have enumerated can be applied, at least in this hypothetical case.

EXHIBIT 5

RESPONSIBILITIES FOR MAKING A SALE

Sales Office	Distributing Point	
X		Obtains correct order from salesman.
X		Obtains rating from credit department; assistance in special terms of financing according to company policy (if necessary).
X		Prepares acknowledgment of order, notice to distributing point, invoice.
	X	Obtains route and rate from traffic department (if necessary).
	X	Prepares bill of lading, packing slip, notice of shipment to customer and sales office.
	X	Makes correct shipment.
X		Mails invoice to customer.
X		Maintains trade account file of open orders and invoices.
X		Receives or collects and deposits payment.
X		Makes daily report to accounting department of amounts of open orders, invoices, and receipts.
X		Notifies collections department when any payments are overdue (if necessary).

There is no question as to where responsibility rests in the revised procedure. The sales office is responsible for the order, the credit risk, the invoice, and the collection. It is responsible for adherence to company policy on credit and collections. All these are aspects of customer relations, and the effect of the procedure is to centralize responsibility for them in the line marketing organization.

The distributing point is responsible for the shipping papers, delivery means, and compliance with the order. These are all allied functions.

Credit, collection, and traffic are used for their specialized knowledge in special cases. Billing is decentralized. The work of accounts receivable is reduced because receivables are recorded by sales office totals. If more detailed sales information is required, copies of invoices can be transmitted internally to provide it.

Costs would be higher in sales offices to the extent that preparing orders, mailing invoices, maintaining a trade account file, and making collections, deposits, and daily financial reports are new functions. Costs would be reduced in sales, credit, traffic, collections, and accounting. Three-way phone calls would be largely eliminated. Impedance to prompt completing action would be reduced, as would the potential for errors and delays.

The purpose of this review of a case in procedures is to establish an approach to this type of problem in general. There are situations of this sort to be found in any sizable company. If they do not relate to making a sale, they may be located in the requisitioning-purchasing-receiving-inventory procedure, or in that for capital projects-procurement-property records, or in charge-payroll-paying procedures. Whenever paperwork passes through several organizational units, the process should be analyzed. It would be a rare case that could not stand some simplification and cost reduction.

In addition to simplification of the flow of paperwork, attention should be given redundant collection, dissemination, and retention of information. You are quite likely to find, for example, a number of different organizational units retaining overlapping data on your salaried personnel. The salaried payroll unit will have salary and deduction data. Similar records may be kept by pension, insurance, and tax units. Personnel will have records on salary progression. Medical keeps personal histories of annual physicals. The bonus and extra compensation unit, organization planners, military security unit, and management development group will have files on key personnel. All these groups analyze, interpret, and summarize their work; this information, needless to say, is contained in periodic reports to other groups. It would take considerable investigation just to count up the number of times your name is typed on reports and records during a year in the course of all this work.

The point, of course, is the amount of redundant information collected, recompiled periodically, stored, and reworked. The basic data could all be stored on tapes and coded for the particular purposes of most of the groups named. While the salary area may be a poor place to start cutting down redundant records, it illustrates the type of condition to look for.

Of greater concern is the amount of information flowing

in parallel channels all having similar content. Production, sales, and financial people are all likely to be collecting similar data on product costs, inventories, packaging costs, warehouse stocks. Each wants to be able to report on the situation in his own way, and each requires data in slightly different form. Their requirements impose a considerable burden on accountants and clerks in lower echelons.

In this connection, it is well to look at the policies and procedures drawn up by your functional staff departments to guide lower echelons. Because they emanate from headquarters as company policy, they can become as sacrosanct as IRS regulations. Probably, they impose costs—and organizational rigidity—some of which will seem excessive from the executive point of view.

All procedural areas should be subjected to objective reappraisal from time to time. They are a substantial cost, most of which is indeterminable. They add to organizational inertia. In themselves, few are a direct contribution to making a profit from the manufacture and sale of product.

Use of Staff in Overhead Control

Any serious attempt at overhead control is more than a one-man job. The executive in charge will need to have other hands and brains to study, analyze, and work out details. However, he should not attempt to delegate the problem away, thereby adding another increment to overhead. Rather, he should use staff for specific tasks when and as needed.

When overhead is viewed in toto from the executive

level, it seems like a large amorphous mass. There are all those staff and functional supporting groups. There are all their counterparts at divisional, factory, and cost-center levels. There is the large sum of money that all this costs. Even though that sum is broken up under convenient labels like accounting, advertising, and divisional overhead, it is hard to relate the necessity of it all to the business of making money. On the other hand, everyone charging to overhead is working hard at something or other. All those functions have to be performed; how could you ever run a business without accounting, advertising, or divisional overhead? Yet look at the cost! See what it costs this year as against five or ten years ago. There were accounting, advertising, and divisional overhead then too. Why does it have to cost so much more now? Everyone you talk to, though, can explain at length all he is doing and how much more he really should be doing if he were not understaffed and did not have to live within a budget.

If many executives do not get beyond this point in controlling overhead, it is quite understandable. There is no problem more frustrating—so frustrating, in fact, that many executives prefer to change targets and shoot for another increment of volume to avoid confronting the problem of overhead.

If he persists, however, the first problem of the executive in charge of overhead is to establish who, in all this number of people, is doing what. What reports are being generated? What information is being collected? What are those piles of paperwork being routed through departments and sections? How many people are doing each of those individual functions the departments claim as their responsibilities? How many people do the divisions have performing their own individual support functions? The executive scrutinizing overhead has to get a definition of these things so that he can start sorting out the problems he faces.

To get this first definition, he needs no special staff. He can ask each of the departments and divisions to perform a self-audit: what work, functions, processes, and procedures its people are performing. He can get a description of each task, the number of people required to perform it, and their total annual salary. This overhead stock taking will accomplish several purposes:

- It will uncover the amount of effort now being expended and provide a measure of the cost of such procedures as our example in order processing.

- It will raise in his mind questions about some areas that he will want to investigate further.

- It will give him the basic information he needs in considering trade-offs between one area and another when it becomes necessary to select between areas of expense.

- It will force a certain amount of self-appraisal on department and division heads.

- It will give him information necessary in planning an investigation of overhead areas.

For the investigation itself, however, the responsible executive will have to get assistance. Investigating the ramifications of order completion, for instance, is a project in itself. It can require the knowledge of specialists in several disciplines: cost analysis, office methods, data processing, systems design, industrial engineering, customer relations—to name some. Other areas to be investigated will require different combinations of talents. He will want to avoid creating a new permanent overhead staff to investigate overhead areas. He will want to limit the investigation in terms of time and cost, and he will want to get positive results.

Because of these considerations, many companies organize an overhead study as a project and use the project team or task force approach. They borrow personnel from existing departments. The people they borrow work together as a team and report to the responsible executive.

In setting up such a team, there are several considerations to keep in mind. All the team members must be indoctrinated to insure that they drop departmental loyalties and work objectively for the benefit of the company as a whole. In other words, they must be taught to adopt the executive point of view. They must understand that each discipline is to have equal voice, even though one man may be selected as team leader. Any differences that they cannot reconcile have to be referred to their executive contact for arbitration. They must be extremely tactful in all their organizational contacts. They must gather information without projecting their individual points of view. They must never imply criticism of people or procedures they are investigating. The time to criticize and to develop alternatives is after they have gathered the facts on what is being done.

All this is rather easy to accomplish. Nearly all employees will like being assigned to work with one of the executives of the company. They will appreciate the opportunity to share his point of view. They will like the specific nature and objectives of their assignment. They will appreciate the opportunity to demonstrate their abilities under such circumstances. They will complete their work with a feeling of accomplishment, even if their recommendation is to continue an existing practice. Moreover, the whole experience will add to their capabilities.

It must be understood from the first by all concerned that the team itself makes no changes. Its sole function is to study and recommend. Any change is made by executive action, whether by decree or by persuasion.

It is easy to see why companies that have used this approach are well satisfied with the results. Unless a company has perfect procedures—and what company does?—the project team approach is almost certain to develop improvements in existing systems. It is usually the case that the result is both a better system and less cost. An executive who can list such an achievement can be justly proud of his accomplishment.

Authorization of Overhead Expenses

Proper authorization procedures are a necessary step in clarifying responsibility for overhead and establishing unified accountability. Admittedly, this is easier to say than to accomplish. Nevertheless, it is an essential part of overhead control.

It is safe to generalize about most companies that the

bulk of their overhead expenses was never properly authorized. Who, for example, ever authorized the procedure for making a sale that we have just analyzed? It got started somewhere. It grew as the number of orders increased. At some stage it was agreed that the credit department should get a look at orders in an effort to cut down on bad accounts. At another time it was argued that traffic should make a study of freight bills. When the collection department was formed, the sales department concurred— there was no use having it if it were not going to be used. Each of these activities had to justify itself at budget time, especially when it had to add personnel to be able to process increasing volume. Looking back on it now, however, you can see that a number of incremental decisions must have been made without any proper evaluation of their effect on the organization or on overhead. Nevertheless, no one was given an opportunity to authorize the activity that is actually going on. No one knew or does know what that activity really costs. No one had the chance to decide that this was better than other ways of applying gross profit.

As already indicated, overhead expenses come about for a number of reasons:

- An organizational unit is created, perhaps as an experiment, to perform a function. It must be given an initial budget in order to begin to do its job. By the time it is reviewed, it has developed a rationale for existence and, quite possibly, for expansion of its activity.
- Someone starts circulating through the different

departments a proposition that consideration be given to having "someone"—normally, the writer —perform some new activity. When he gets reactions back, and none is strenuously negative, he starts the proposed activity "on a trial basis."

- It is found that proper attention to a previously neglected function results in dramatic examples of cost savings, and a new group is formed to pursue the function. As usual, the savings become less and less dramatic. In fact, the major cost saving has been achieved by the initial study, and the new group is largely a new built-in cost. Meantime, the function has become so intermeshed in company procedures that it seems necessary to the company's existence. In fact, the company may lose the capability of operating without it (as in the case of computers).

- Then there is the case of an under-employed specialist who manufactures an activity and builds up a certain demand for his reports or services.

All these things happen even though the budget committee is very rough on the heads of overhead departments and is quite firm in holding the line. However, it cannot very well disband an activity that is claimed to be saving more than it costs or another that is approved by all the departments or another that is performing a real service. Since budget review is really just a sideline for the committee members, they are hardly in a position to reject opinions of other people who should know so much more than they of the details of company operations, Reluctantly, therefore, they go along again this year, after making a few superficial cuts to show that they mean business. Unfortunately, experience in many companies demonstrates that overhead expenses cannot be controlled by this means. A necessary element in the control program is control of authorization to spend.

If a proper system of charging for use is established, there is no particular difficulty in controlling overhead categories of counseling and services. No accountable employee will authorize an amount of charges in these categories which he cannot defend. Primary problems are:

- To provide periodic review and confirmation of standing authorizations so that, if expenses get out of line, authorization can be rescinded. If such review is not provided—and exercised—subordinates may develop the idea that it is policy to use the service even if they could operate just as well without it.

- To avoid divided responsibility for authorizations. If too many approvals must be collected before the necessary signature is put on an authorization, no one is really responsible and authorization becomes a mere formality. Ideally, only two people should be officially involved in the authorization process: (1) the direct user of the service and (2) his line superior. Any higher-level authorization should be by way of the normal budgetary approval.

- To require advance planning for overhead services in terms of periodic forecasts of use by those to whom expenses are to be charged. Such forecasts, in turn, can be converted into budgets by those who are to supply the services. In this way, stability of operations can be assured to overhead departments.

It is a problem of the first order, however, to establish a system of authorization in the general overhead category. These are companywide expenses—those of executives and executive staff, of idle time of overhead departments, and of services not directly chargeable to profit centers or other departments. For all these expenses only the executive is responsible, and accountability for them occurs only in profit and loss statements for the company as a whole.

It is scarcely possible to lay down rules for authorizing general overhead that would be applicable to most companies. Operations at this level in particular are too much a reflection of the individual styles of principal executives to allow establishment of universal procedures. At best, some guidelines can be mentioned that can be adapted to individual situations.

We have already discussed the executive attitude that must prevail if there is to be a successful program of overhead control. What is accomplished at all subordinate levels will reflect this attitude. If there is careful consideration of expenses here, other echelons can be expected to follow the example. Part of the necessary consideration is a form of authorization of expenses for which only the executive can bear responsibility.

Someone at the executive level must have overhead expenses as a primary concern and must have primary responsibility for them. As with other things, overhead control will not receive adequate and consistent attention if it is treated as a minor interest at the executive level. That is the failing of executive budget committees. They are regarded as an interruption of primary responsibilities. Everyone hastens away from them with relief when the last budget has been reviewed and approved.

To preclude such an attitude in the overhead area, the organization has to know that some one executive has responsibility for overhead expenses. He must regard them as a primary responsibility, not merely as an assignment to be discharged when budget time comes around. Among other things, he must act as the "executive conscience" in this area. Through him the executive attitude toward overhead expenses will be reflected and applied not only to subordinate overhead departments but also to executive actions. He should be the formal authorizer of general overhead expenses. As mentioned earlier, he should be subordinate only to the principal executive in matters of overhead expenses and the supervision of overhead departments.

Obviously this is not a position in which to gain popularity. Its incumbent will have to scrutinize pet projects, both of executives and of overhead departments. To much of the organization he will seem always to be negative. Nevertheless, it will not be difficult for him to save the company money. To do so, however, he will have to have the firm support of the principal executive and the understanding of his fellow executives. He need not be popular to be effective.

Even he will not be able to establish a system for nipping procedures in the bud. However, he will be in a position to analyze and reform those that encumber operations of the company. With authority to approve budgets of overhead departments and to authorize general overhead expenses, he becomes the source of overhead control which is the element most companies lack.

Elimination of Positions

Any serious attempt at overhead control will mean elimination of some positions. Reducing the funding of some functions to strengthen others and, even more, simplification of procedures will uncover areas that are overstaffed. The resulting personnel problems should be anticipated.

The crisis approach to overhead control is usually characterized by severe demoralization of the organization, loss of some employees the company was planning to retain, and reduction of initiative on the part of the remainder. One of the reasons for these phenomena is that terminations start before anyone has really thought out how they should be handled. The result, to outsiders and insiders alike, is as though the hatchet had been unsheathed and used brutally. The only way to avoid this impression is to foresee the possibility of terminations, to plan carefully how they are to be handled, and to prepare the organization for application of the plan. To do these things properly, the responsible executive must know something about the psychology of those in staff and supporting positions.

Many parts of this book must seem like criticism of overhead employees. It was not meant to be that way. For one thing, the writer has spent many years in staff positions. While a few in such positions develop, as Koontz and O'Donnell point out,[2] an attitude of arrogance toward other parts of the organization, most are sincerely desirous of serving the other departments and contributing to the success of the company.

Indeed, nearly all employees in these positions are sincere servants of the firm. Within the limits of their positions, they will go out of their way to provide assistance to others. They like to attribute importance to the function they are performing, and they constantly seek ways of doing it better. Because of the specialized nature of their functions, probably their entire careers have been spent working in a single area. In that time, they have acquired depth of knowledge, increased competence, and great pride in their work.

To such dedicated servants, it can come only as a psychological shock to contemplate the possibility that the company may curtail or discontinue performance of their functions and, in the process, their own careers. Common justice demands that this shock be anticipated and every effort be made to assist them in making the transition they

[2] Harold Koontz and Cyril O'Donnell, *Principles of Management,* McGraw-Hill Book Co., Inc., New York, 1964.

face. Indeed, many companies go to seemingly unprecedented lengths to help them adjust to the new situation. Among the provisions that have been made are:

- Special arrangements for early retirement for those not qualifying by age or length of service under the company plan.
- Retention of pension rights until retirement age even though service is terminated.
- The hiring of placement services to obtain suitable new employment.
- Assistance in relocation to a new job.
- Special termination pay.

In actuality, every employee has individual problems and potentials for adjustment. It is best, therefore, to develop a set of options which can be drawn on in personnel counseling to fit individual cases. No doubt, maximum limits will be necessary. Flexibility within them, however, will permit selection of the most suitable type of assistance for each individual.

Among the options that should be considered is the possibility of serving the company in a completely different capacity, if there is a likely opening, even though the employee may lack the qualifications the position description specifies. People have great latent capacity for rising to meet a challenge if they can see a future, however different from the one they have contemplated, and an opportunity for accomplishment. This option may be hard for your personnel people to take seriously because they are accustomed to pinpointing a man to a job. Nevertheless, business history is replete with the successes of men

105

not obviously qualified in the areas where they finally realized their true potential.

One further option to consider is to give the employee an opportunity to make a place for himself, still within the company, of his choosing. Many employees nurse the ambition to prove themselves in an area other than the one they are in. Some may have the latent capacity to do so.

In any case, the plan for termination cannot lessen the psychological shock to the employee. It should seek, however, to replace that condition as soon as possible with a new future which he will see as an opportunity.

Supervision of Overhead

To a considerable degree, proper supervision of overhead is a reflection of proper definition of responsibility for overhead charges. However, executive supervision of general overhead is almost entirely in terms of planning, budgeting, measuring accomplishment, and monitoring performance in those terms.

Two types of supervision are involved in the control of overhead. First, there is the type of supervision used in profit and cost centers. Second, there is the type required in the management of general overhead.

Normally, managers of profit and cost centers are charged with the overheads associated with their own indirect costs. An example would be a factory production scheduling group. These managers may also require supporting counseling and services from overhead departments in order to perform their operations. For instance, the factory manager may need engineering assistance in designing an addition to the building, such assistance being available from an overhead department.

It is usual practice to delegate to managers at these levels control over their own direct costs, subject to monitoring and review by higher echelons. They are expected to schedule labor and facilities and to control the utilization of materials and power. Their effectiveness in these managerial responsibilities is measured by periodic performance reports. In most companies, their superiors do not attempt to dictate to them in these areas of direct costs. In fact, it would usually be considered more proper to replace a manager whose performance in controlling direct costs was inadequate than to superimpose such control from above.

Practice in regard to the delegation of control of overheads is less uniform. In actuality, subordinate managers are as able to schedule their own indirect as well as their direct workers. They are equally capable of using overhead counseling and services effectively. They are generally more effective than higher echelons in keeping their overheads in line with their direct costs. From the standpoint of controlling overhead, therefore, it is desirable to make an effective delegation to subordinate managers of control over their own overheads. To do so, the following guidelines should be adhered to by their superiors:

1. Subordinate managers must be informed as to any criteria, beyond those of periodic financial reports, by which their performance is to be judged. If

the manager of a cost center believes he is to be judged solely on cost, for instance, he may violate an overall company policy which requires him to provide adequate safety training of personnel.

2. Except for any general company policies, he should be free to make his own work assignments to his own overhead personnel. He should have flexibility in using his staff, not only for economy but also for the benefit of his employees in developing their capabilities.

3. Except for essential policy constraints, he should be given free choice to use or not to use overhead departments which provide supporting services. The manager of a branch plant, for example, probably can get the foundation design for an addition cheaper and better locally than it can be obtained from a central engineering department.

4. A subordinate manager should have the authority to proceed with an overhead expense as he sees fit if he has had the foresight to project it in his budget and if he has received approval of his budget from his immediate superior. The superior has the responsibility to see that subordinate budgets are submitted for approval at the executive level where all such budgets can be incorporated in company projections.

5. The subordinate manager should be equally free to proceed with a special item of expense once he has had approval from his immediate superior. The latter is responsible to evaluate the effect of

a special expense on his own budget and, if he does not have provision for it, to obtain special executive approval.

6. All the indirect costs he controls should be charged to the subordinate manager as incurred and should appear on his performance reports so that he is constantly reminded of the direct connection between his overhead expenses and his total costs or between his overhead and his profit.

If these criteria are met, control of overhead that is in support of line production and sales can be successfully delegated. Subordinate managers will know where they stand and what their authority is. Their overall performance will be brought, as far as possible, into periodic performance reports, which remain the most objective standard we have for judging results of either our own performance or that of subordinates. To the extent that there are areas of performance not measured in accounting reports—for example, in respect to safety and housekeeping—superiors have the responsibility to see that subordinates receive adequate training and that their performance is monitored and supervised. This may place on the superior the obligation to provide in his own overhead budget for overhead services of specialists to conduct training and auditing of subordinates. Control of overhead, therefore, is not only clamping down on expenses. It is also the application of expenses to strengthen the performance of the line. This, after all, is the fundamental purpose in having overhead: to make the line more effective in the manufacture and sale of product.

This statement applies even in the area of general overhead, where specialized functions often seem to assume the character of separate entities having their own validity irrespective of their essentiality to the line. If this characteristic appears strongly in overhead departments, it is because an adequate system for controlling and supervising overhead does not exist. The control system itself has the effect of structuring overhead so that cost and control bear on the organization where use is made of it. The area of general overhead, however, remains largely amorphous, and it is here that executive supervision assumes a special character.

Supervision of profit centers includes not only responsibility for monitoring their financial performance but also the obligation to stimulate them with new outlooks on products and markets. The responsible executive has to find challenges which will inspire those who manage profit centers to raise their sights and seek more difficult targets. It gains nothing to that enterprise, however, for the responsible executive to seek special ways for overhead departments to provide additional services to, and lay more cost on, the already burdened profit centers.

The point has already been made that supervision of general overhead is, in itself, a special executive function. The importance and special nature of this function require structuring of the executive level to accomplish it. We will assume that general overhead is to be supervised by an executive chief of staff and go on to discuss his role and some of his problems.

The executive for overhead has to supervise a great

diversity of activity. He cannot rely on his own knowledge, therefore, either to manage the activities of overhead departments or to speak for them in executive circles. He cannot expect to tell the general counsel how to defend a suit, direct the controller on the accounting system to use, or draw up a research program. It is in the specialized nature of overhead functions that they must be conducted by those performing them, at least insofar as they are of a professional character. Supervision of these areas, then, is different from supervision in the lines of manufacturing and sales, where organizational level is normally equivalent to depth of experience in that line.

In the same way, the executive for overhead abuses his position if he attempts to counsel others in the company in regard to the functions under his purview. No matter what his background, obviously he cannot have the intensity of knowledge of those whose entire vocation is the law, accounting, or research.

Nevertheless, he can provide the essential management link required by both the principal executive and the overhead departments. Up to this point, we have considered mostly the financial aspects of this relationship. They are at the heart of the problem of control and the principal element in supervision. They are the areas in which the executive for overhead must be a competent manager: He is the one to whom they look for company projections, for budget approvals, and for performance reviews. In turn, he is their source of authority to spend, once their plans have been approved. He is, likewise, the one to whom the principal executive turns for information and recommendations in matters of overhead expense, and in that area he is expected to speak with authority. He is the instrument through which the executive effects changes in overhead expenses.

But the position is broader than this brief description of matters we have discussed before. Overhead departments look to him, also, as the source of company policy in its effects on them, the interpreter of company plans insofar as they affect their own planning, and their executive contact for adjudication of interdepartmental matters in which they have a position. He is the point at which they apply pressure on the executive for innovations that they think will benefit the company. He is the source of studies and analyses of more efficient ways to perform overhead functions, particularly in the troublesome area of overlapping procedures. In the event that reduction of overhead becomes necessary, he is the enforcer of the company plan.

The executive for overhead can expect to be exposed to two opposing forces in his work: (1) the need to delegate responsibility as the enterprise becomes larger and more complex, as opposed to (2) the desire to centralize control over the performance of functions at subordinate levels. While these two forces involve the broad areas of organizational structure, communication, and supervision, they also enter directly into the problem of executive responsibility for general overhead.

As we have seen in the case of making a sale, simplification of an overlapping procedure results in clarification of responsibility. Consequently, more of the entire process could be delegated to a lower level. The same principle, applied here in miniature, goes on continually as a company evolves. In a small company, control of costs is lodged in the principal executive. As the company grows, responsibility is delegated to one or more cost centers. Such delegation is inevitable as the number and complexity of matters to be dealt with exceed his capacity for work. With further growth, the primary delegation is to profit centers, composed of groups of cost centers. In the final step, seen in the largest companies, delegation is to groups of profit centers. Throughout this evolutionary process, complexity is reduced and the scope of work brought within human proportions by simplification of organizational structure and further delegation of responsibility.

As an activity becomes further removed from the purview of the executive level through this process of delegation, there is an increasing tendency to assume (whenever a problem arises in connection with it) that this activity is out of control. Perhaps an executive receives a telephone call from one of his business friends who mentions, in passing, that his last shipment was all mixed up. His reaction is likely to be that his staff should "get a better handle on this." After meetings and study groups have considered the matter, a whole new overlapping procedure is instituted. To the extent that it duplicates the faults we have found in such procedures, it will result primarily in added organizational complexity, dilution of responsibility, and increased cost.

Curiously enough, it will not really result in better control. Neither the executive nor those who have got a better handle on it are checking the forms now flowing through the hands of clerks in their departments. Mistakes can still occur. Probably, the chance of their occurrence has increased because of the number of times forms are transcribed and facts are posted. However, there is a *feeling* of better control because the department manager can actually see activity around him without the necessity of going to a subordinate level or a branch location and checking on it. He can make reassuring reports on that activity to the executive level.

This process of centralization is especially apparent in regard to overhead functions. Those in charge of such functions feel that they are left out and are not discharging their responsibility if they are not aware of activities having any bearing on their functions wherever they are performed. Hence, lower echelons are required to supply them with periodic reports, copies of forms, and special reports which they, in turn, can reprocess into reports to the executive and other departments.

The tendency to centralization of this type has become greater in recent years with general acceptance of the cost of high-speed communication. It has become exaggerated latterly in some companies with the use of computers. Once a company has equipped itself to get the information and has the means to process, store, and report it, there is an almost irreversible pressure to use it. The attitude prevails that we have the tielines and we have the computer capacity; therefore, we should use them. This is equivalent to a production man saying that we have the enamel on hand; therefore, we should put an extra coat of finish on this run of product.

To a greater or lesser degree, this tendency to centralization exists in respect to all types of functions. It is nourished, all too often, by faulty estimates of cost. The executive for overhead has to develop the ability to recognize when centralization is undermining delegation and which should prevail in each instance. He will learn when centralization is being urged under the guise of cost savings and how to make his own analyses of costs. In these respects, he can make a positive contribution to his company, providing balance and continuity in the executive philosophy. While at first he may be regarded as the hatchet man, in the end he should be recognized as a principal source of strength and stability in the development of the company.

He can best gain this recognition by realizing from the start that he must be a restraining influence without destroying the initiative of those he is supervising. He must encourage creative thinking at the same time that he is practicing control. He must develop, not only in himself but also in those supervising overhead and charged with overhead, the philosophy that the disposition of gross profit to expenses is a problem in selectivity. When they advance something new, he must help them weigh the respective merits of new versus old. He should try to stimulate them to develop new concepts good enough that they are willing to sacrifice something to get them. At the same time, he should evaluate in his own mind which one, of all the activities being supported, might be traded off to make way for a new activity.

Supervision of overhead, therefore, is not as negative a

function as may at first be supposed. It must provide control of aggregate expenditures, but, within that limit, it can assist greatly in development of the organization along more effective lines.

Overhead Profit Center

Some companies have gone much further than others in developing the profit motivation of those in functions not directly related to producing and selling. Techniques are available that can be applied more widely to accomplish this purpose.

One of the more effective ways to keep the problem of general overhead under executive consideration is to turn the corporate headquarters into a profit center. Admittedly this is a fiction, but it is in keeping with the common concept that a corporation can be divided up into a number of profit centers. This too is a fiction that has been adopted successfully by many corporations.

To turn the head office into a profit center, it must have revenues. The way some companies have approached this situation is to say that the company will charge profit centers for financing or for corporate management. A corporation, in fact, has expenses of which the managers of profit centers may not even be aware; for instance, the annual fee for listing on the New York Stock Exchange. Furthermore, managers of profit centers are entrusted with assets which they are to exploit for the benefit of the stockholders.

116

A charge on profit centers for financing or for corporate management therefore constitutes a much more rational basis for levying a fee on them than does a straightforward allocation to cover general overhead. Such a fee[3] is logically based on investment in net fixed assets, accounts receivable, and inventory, sometimes weighted with a percentage of total salaries.

The corporate headquarters expenses are those of the executive establishment plus overhead expenses not chargeable directly to profit centers. Thus the corporate headquarters can have both revenues and expenses, and the balance can be said to represent a profit or loss to its own account.

This approach has several advantages over the more common method of allocating overhead. It is generally more understandable to the managers of profit centers. They can accept readily the need for a financial charge, provided it is not seriously in excess of commercial bank rates. They derive the feeling that they can control the amount they are charged through their use of assets and their control of inventories and receivables, while they can only complain about an allocation. Furthermore, such an approach puts incentives on them in the right direction: to control the amount of investment they are using. They can accept, also, a small percentage charge for corporate management functions.

More important, this approach ties general overhead

[3] For examples see Carl G. Baumes, *Allocating Corporate Expenses,* Studies in Business Policies No. 108, National Industrial Conference Board, New York, 1963.

directly into the profit system. No chief executive would like to admit to his subordinate managers that he cannot strike a favorable balance between his own revenues and costs. He would not like to admit that he has to charge more than bank rates for financing. He would not want to say that he cannot keep expenses in line with income, in good times and bad.

Consequently, this approach does a great deal to insure a consistent attitude toward general overhead at the executive level. It permits the adoption of the same methods of forecasting and reporting of variances used in the operating profit centers. While everyone will think of the fictional aspects of the system before it is adopted, he will be confronted afterward with the common phenomenon that numbers acquire a validity of their own once they are written down and that profits are something to strive for at all levels in the company.

There is no reason, in principle, why any or all overhead functions should not be put on a profit-center basis. This, in effect, is what some of the oil companies have done in creating shipping and pipeline subsidiaries: They have made profit centers of activities whose primary reason for being was to supply services to their other profit centers. Once established, such subsidiaries quickly seek to solidify their positions by obtaining revenues from external as well as internal sources. Likewise, export departments of many companies are set up as profit centers.

If a company has an effective system for direct-charging the costs of overhead functions, such charges could be regarded as revenues. Since each function would have cost and income, it could be reported in the form of a profit and loss statement. However, we could expect every overhead function to seek some means of developing external sources of income. While such activity would have an important effect on the motivation of people in these overhead profit centers, the diversity of problems it would bring to the executive level would take a great deal of attention away from the older profit centers. The problems associated with successful development of service businesses would seem alien to those whose careers had been in a manufacturing industry.

For these reasons, the wholesale conversion of overhead departments into profit centers is not advocated. Important as it is to develop profit motivation in those performing support functions, the attendant stresses on the organization may be too severe to make this approach successful for most companies if it is adopted wholesale. Where appropriate, however, it merits consideration in overhead planning.

Some Conclusions

When the overhead rate of a company gets too high, it provides a signal that, for the present level of business, an imbalance exists between those activities that are supposed to generate profits—manufacturing and selling—and those that are merely ancillary to the profit-making process. It is easy to explain away that signal; our easy rationalization these days is that it will be taken care of by greater volume next year. The signal (even if it is erased by greater volume next year) nevertheless indicates basic imbalance in the organization which wise management must recognize.

The first corrective to be applied is the restructuring of overhead so that those functions which, in fact, are in direct support of profit centers become subsidiary to them. The manager of a profit center will fight harder for a good record on his performance reports than he will for the maintenance of an inflated level of overhead support. The remaining part of general overhead must be brought under direct executive supervision. If the executive then favors an artificially high level of overhead activity, it will be quite clear where responsibility lies. Furthermore, the remedy will not be far to seek, and it will be readily determined to what extent the enterprise can be made profitable again.

In any case, no responsible management will risk prolongation of a low profit level in order to favor the very parts of overhead which are least contributory; that is, maintenance of empire and preoccupation with procedural matters. Any management may well have a bias in favor of more advertising or engineering, research or marketing. Such a bias is defensible only to the extent that it supports more creative and professional activity for the future benefit of the enterprise. It is for the executive, then, to defend such an emphasis on those grounds. Overhead for its own sake is indefensible. To the extent that it does not contribute directly to profit centers, or is not an investment in creative activity for the future of the company, it is a luxury that the competition, if not the stockholders, will not permit.

The implication of these conclusions is that the structuring of overhead in order to enhance a function is both poor organization and faulty policy. Too many companies take authority away from the line in order to give top-to-bottom responsibility for a functional area to an overhead department. In the long run, one way or another, the function will have to be restructured for the contribution it can make to the enterprise. That part which is in direct support of immediate profit making has to become part of the organization subordinate to profit centers. That part which is a corporate investment in the future has to become an organizational responsibility of the executive.

We have been led away from this approach in our desire to see greater efficiency in the performance of overhead functions. Centralization of such functions means that a higher quality of personnel and more advanced equipment can be justified. No matter what the apparent gain in efficiency, for many companies it has been more than offset by proportionately higher total cost. It is more important to control the total cost of overhead than it is to gain more efficiency in its performance.

Gains in efficiency through centralization, furthermore, relate almost entirely to the procedural aspects of overhead functions. They do little to enhance the creative aspects of advertising, engineering, research, or marketing. For the great ideas and discoveries we are still dependent on the abilities of human beings—and the more sources of ideas and inventions the better.

Many of the gains in procedural activity that we appear to have made are largely illusory. The illusion comes about, to a great extent, because we lose sight of the purposes of procedures and confuse activity with accomplishment. Many of these procedural activities have come about because we have also allowed overhead specialists to assume responsibilities which properly belong on the line. The line, after all, will continue to focus on the main objective: to show a satisfactory profit. If someone else wants to do the advertising or engineering or research, why—those are side issues.

The result is that we take functions away from line departments instead of crowding more responsibility onto them. This is a process that has gone far enough in most companies and should be reversed. The reward for success in showing a profit should be more responsibility. We should give line managers more scope to exercise their abilities by giving them more direct control over functions intended to support their profit-making activities. What we are too likely to do is to dilute a line manager's authority by putting more things in the category of charges allocated to him.

Finally, we should abandon the common practice of putting good line men into staff positions when we do not have an immediate assignment for them. Far too many of them are successful in making careers for themselves as staff men, but we pay for those careers instead of gaining directly from them. Perhaps these men would be equally successful in making new profits for us if we gave them the chance to find new products, new markets, or new ways for us to do business. Any new addition to overhead should be considered as seriously as a capital investment, and this is one such addition that we could avoid if we challenge our own management ability.

In any case, overhead is not something to worry about once every few years. Making money is more exciting than conserving money, but both are essential business functions. It is necessary to make a profit. It is just as necessary to apply profit wisely. Overhead, therefore, is an aspect of management that should be considered as consistently as the monthly profit statement because that is where the results of controlling overhead are to be found.

About the Author

HARRY TIPPER, JR. is an executive assistant at Hercules Powder Company, specializing in problems of general management, including corporate organization and measurement and control of costs. He was educated at Princeton University.

Following World War II Mr. Tipper joined John B. Pierce Foundation, eventually becoming assistant executive director. He has also served as manager of the Building Research Laboratories of Southwest Research Institute and sales promotion manager of Construction Service Company, and he was assistant to the president of Young Development Laboratories when they were merged into Hercules Powder Company.

Mr. Tipper is author of one previous book and a number of articles, and he has served as editor of an export trade paper. His broad background encompasses the management of scientific research, foreign trade, advertising, and public relations. More recently, he has concentrated on the corporate–divisional relationships in large decentralized companies.